TEACHING the Tricky Bits

SCIENCE

Materials

John Stringer

Published by
Hopscotch Educational Publishing Ltd,
29 Waterloo Place,
Leamington Spa CV32 5LA
Tel: 01926 744227

© 2001 Hopscotch Educational Publishing

Written by John Stringer
Series design by Blade Communications
Illustrated by Bernard Connors
Printed by Clintplan, Southam

ISBN 1-902239-70-9

Contents

About the series

Teaching the Tricky Bits arose out of a frustrated teacher's cry for help when one of the children in her class said 'But why do we need blood?' She sort-of knew the answer but couldn't quite explain it so that the child could understand.

And so began the development of a series of books designed to inform non-specialist teachers about the different science topics in the National Curriculum.

But soon we realised that often information on science tends to be dry and can only be taken in in bite-sized pieces for fear of falling asleep. So we agreed that we needed a series of books that would keep teachers informed and awake!

This is what we have achieved. This book, and the other three in the series, all contain vital, useful and fascinating information written by John Stringer, who is adviser to the Channel 4 series 'Fourways Farm' and 'Making Sense of Science', and writer of many primary science resources.

But just as important as the information John has supplied is the approach he has taken with his writing – it's fun to read! There are amusing scenarios and anecdotes. You really won't fall asleep!

Then we realised that it's all well and good having all this information and rolling about in the aisles laughing, but what are you going to do with it? Or, more importantly, what are the children going to do with your new-found knowledge?

So, John has provided relevant activities for each chapter, starting with what could be done at level 1 and going all the way to level 5.

This makes these books ideal for every teacher. You can allocate activities according to ability. You can still use the book if you find yourself teaching a different age group.

We hope you enjoy reading and using this book as much as we have enjoyed putting it together!

Other titles in the series are:

Forces, electricity and magnetism
(and the Earth in space)

ISBN 1 902239 69 5

The Human Body

ISBN 1 902239 68 7

Plants and animals

ISBN 1 902239 71 7

Introduction

The world is full of stuff. In fact, it's made from stuff – including you, me and this book. Scientists call this stuff 'material' – a confusing word if you are five years old and you are taken to buy some material for your bedroom curtains. Because 'material' – in the scientific sense – isn't just fabric. It's all the stuff in the world – rocks, wood,

plastic and steel. It's rare and expensive – like gold and diamonds – or common and cheap, like soil and water. It's everywhere. Different materials have different properties.

By looking at the properties of materials, how they are used and how they might be changed, this subject prepares children for their later understanding of chemistry.

What you need to know

The National Curriculum expects that pupils will learn:

- about the properties of materials
- about grouping materials by their properties
- about the uses of materials, and how we match materials by their properties
- about the ways that materials can be changed – by heating and cooling (Key Stage 1) and burning (Key Stage 2)
- that some of these changes can be reversed
- that some of these changes involve a change in state
- about solutions, and separation by filtration and evaporation.

It is important to tackle work on materials in a logical order like this. Only then can children understand that materials differ; that they can be grouped and classified in many ways; that this classification can help us to choose the right materials for a task; and finally, that there are ways of changing materials that make them suitable for a range of needs and tasks.

What is all this stuff made from?

Let's begin with the bit you can't teach – at least if you teach in a primary school. The National Curriculum (1999) states on page 87 that 'Particle theory does not need to be taught.'

That's a bit sad. Particle theory is simply the idea that everything is made up of very tiny bits, or particles. An understanding of this is enormously helpful when learning about materials – about 'stuff'. And it isn't difficult to understand.

A selection of great and good scientists were asked to imagine that all the science knowledge in the world was to be destroyed but they could save one piece of information. What would it be? Almost without exception, they chose the same idea – rejecting evolution, electricity and Newton's laws of motion. The fact they wanted to pass on to succeeding generations was that all matter is made up of tiny particles.

Words like 'atom', 'molecule' and 'particle' are in general use – sometimes correctly, sometimes not. Most young children could make a stab at explaining what particles are, or at least that they are 'very, very small bits'. Some might even know that they are mostly space. Understanding what particles are is a great help to understanding the behaviour of materials.

Particles everywhere

Everything is made up of particles. The things around you – the Earth itself, plants, animals and your family. You, too.

- If the particles are closely bonded together – able to vibrate but not part from each other – then the material is a solid.

- If the particles are close but not packed, so that they can move around, the material is a liquid.

- If the particles are widely spaced and move around, occasionally crashing into one another, the material is a gas.

These three are called **the states of matter**. Children don't need to know this. What matters is that they understand that the cloudy stuff in the bathroom and the icy stuff in the fridge are both water. Water can exist in three different states, depending on what its particles are doing.

Lighter than water

Water particles bonded together make ice. Unfortunately for the 'Titanic', ice is lighter than water. This is a very unusual but important fact that comes up time and again in this book. It is very unusual for a solid material to weigh less than its liquid. Apart from water, only a material called bismuth behaves like this. (You might have come across this pinkish metal if you have had a gastric ulcer. It is used in soothing medicines.)

Once you understand particle theory, you can understand why this should be. When water freezes, its particles form a kind of cage – a rigid pattern in which the particles are held away from each other. So there is more space in an ice cube than there is in water.

Changes with temperature

The changes between the three states of matter are connected to changes in temperature. Increase the temperature and a solid becomes a liquid, or a liquid a gas. (Very occasionally, a solid becomes a gas without a liquid stage.) Reduce the temperature, and gas becomes a liquid, or a liquid solidifies.

The importance of temperature was known to the Ancient Greeks, and Hero of Alexandria made an early temperature measure called a hermoscope. It was Galileo who made the first air thermometer, but it was his friend Santorio Santorio (yes, twice!) who first used it to measure changes in body temperature during illness and recovery.

Fascinating facts

- There is another state of matter, if you really must know. There is something called plasma in stars and in fluorescent lights. At very high temperatures, atoms in gases collide so fiercely that they are broken up. Bits called electrons, that normally orbit the central nucleus of an atom, are knocked loose. The result is called plasma.

- The smallest particle there can be is called a quark. It got its name from a line in James Joyce's *Finnegan's Wake* – 'Three quarks for Master Marks'. There are six 'flavours' including 'strange' and 'charm', and each flavour has three 'colours': red, blue and green. That means that there are eighteen different 'elementary particles'.

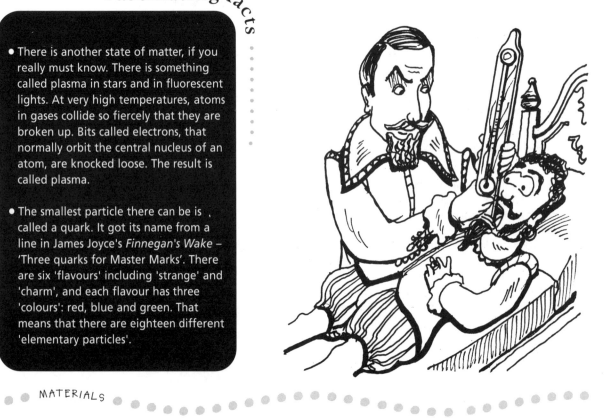

- Early chemistry was concerned with the search for the philosopher's stone. This was a substance that alchemists believed could turn 'base metals' into gold or silver. It could prolong life and cure diseases. The search was a failure, but a lot of interesting discoveries were made on the way.

- Cryogenics is the study of very low temperatures. At these temperatures, food will not decay. Freezing people with terminal illnesses, for revival when a cure is found, is theoretically possible.

- Bullet-proof glass is made from two glass sheets with a resin layer between them. It will crack without shattering.

Absolute zero

However cold it gets, the particles in a solid still move slightly. They may be rigidly held, but they can still vibrate. At the lowest possible temperature – zero degrees Kelvin or, more usually, –273.15 degrees Celsius – this vibration stops. The tiny particles stop moving. It's thought to be impossible to achieve absolute zero; but a temperature two-billionths of a degree above it was produced by Finnish scientists. At this temperature, materials start to behave in strange ways. Liquid helium, for example, usually a gas we use for party balloons, starts to flow uphill. Chemistry is strange stuff.

And glass is a liquid

Let's just get this one out of the way. It comes up later, but it's a favourite in pub quizzes and among well-read children. Glass is a liquid.

Liquids flow. The thicker the liquid, the slower the flow. Wine flows freely while syrup flows slowly. Syrup has a higher viscosity than wine. It takes an age to flow from the tin. But glass has an even higher viscosity than syrup. You can't imagine windows made from syrup. But glass has such a high viscosity – it is so thick – that you can cut it into sheets and put it into windows. Over time, it flows downward. Clear evidence of thickening can be seen at the bottom of century-old windows. The bottom of the pane is thicker than the top.

And in windows not as old as that. A health and safety check at my school recommended that a picture window the size of a billiard table be replaced with a frame and some smaller panes. The glazier approached it with a sledgehammer. I suggested that he could save the pane and cut it into smaller pieces. But the thickening process had already begun, and the old glass was useless for reglazing. I got the school camera just in time to record the crash.

Materials are like that – constantly surprising.

What is a material?

Materials are all around us. They make up every bit of the physical world. They keep us warm, they spill, they pour or squash, they break easily and they can hurt us.

Children learn ways of making materials do what they want them to do – which make a good den or can be shaped into a toy; which are ruined if you leave them out in the rain; which you can combine to make something good to eat.

We experience a wide range of materials in the clothes we wear, the objects we handle and the things we use at home and in school. Some of these materials are natural, and some are made. Some have a long history, and some have been discovered or created very recently. Modern children grow up with a far wider range of materials than they would have encountered a few decades ago. Compared with their Victorian counterparts, they are living in a treasure house of materials of every conceivable colour, texture and shape.

Grouping materials

There are many ways of classifying materials. Here are three of them.

Solid, liquid and gas

Materials can be divided into solids, liquids and gases. This isn't as easy as it sounds. There are some materials that behave in ways that put them in more than one group. Water, for example, can be found in all three states. In addition, it's very hard to prove to children that gases exist. (For more on this, see Chapter 4.)

Natural and artificial

You can also, in theory, divide materials into natural and artificial. Practically speaking, there is a continuum from natural materials (like rock), through worked and shaped materials (like wood and slate), through changed materials (like glass and leather), to materials not found in their pure state (like many metals), to totally artificial materials (such as synthetics like plastics and artificial fibres).

Use

Finally, you can divide materials by use. It isn't always obvious why we choose certain materials for certain uses – though it is when we use glass for windows! We sometimes use materials in direct contravention of their apparent suitability, for example furniture made from paper or diary covers made from circuit boards!

For the purposes of this chapter let's organise the materials into natural and artificial. Sounds easy, doesn't it?

Natural and artifical

The line between materials that are natural and those that are artificial is hard to draw. Any material, once used, becomes artificial in some way. Think of examples – the rocks in a dry-stone wall, the slates on a roof, wood and straw. Wool is a natural material, but needs to be worked to make it usable. Other materials are clearly artificial, such as most metals and all alloys. Some are synthetic, such as plastics and artificial fibres, and are built up from smaller units.

The term 'man-made' is used in some books. This term is often regarded as sexist and the word 'artificial' is an acceptable alternative. However, you can also talk about materials being 'made'. This is an easier word for younger children and its meaning is perfectly clear.

However, labelling with this word is a tricky area. Some objects – shaped, baked or changed in some other way – may be of natural origins, but sliding towards being 'made'. Wood, for example, is a natural material. It would seem straightforward to teach children about it. But beware! You need to explain to the children that wood products have usually been treated and worked. They are on the scale between being natural and 'made' – unless they are driftwood sculpture!

Natural materials

Wool

Wool is a natural material, but we don't use it just as it is cut from the animal. Wool has to be changed before it is used. A sheep's thick wool coat is cut without hurting the sheep. The oily, matted wool is washed and carded – the wool strands are all made to go in the same direction. The carded wool is spun so that the strands make a thread. The threads can be dyed different colours. The wool threads are put together in different ways. They can be pressed together to make felt, knotted together to make knitting or woven together to make cloth. The woven cloth can be cut, sewn and made into clothing. It can be mixed with other fibres, including artifical ones, or treated with finishes, including oil.

Oil

There have been tiny plants and animals in the sea for millions of years. Dead plants and animals sink to the bottom and are covered by sand and mud. As the mud piles up, the bodies are buried and squashed.

It takes millions of years of squashing to change the dead bodies to oil. The oil is in the rock like water in a sponge. The Earth's rocks are always on the move – slowly. They are pushing and pulling at each other as they move a few centimetres each year. When these movements oppose each other, the rocks are pushed up, making a fold. Oil is lighter than most rock, and it moves up until it is trapped by a cap of solid rock. We can drill through to reach the trapped oil. Crude oil is a natural material.

But oil is the natural product that is used to make the artificial material plastic!

Fascinating facts

- There aren't great pools of oil under the Earth. Oil and gas bearing rocks contain between just 5 and 25 per cent oil or gas.

- It takes 3,600 litres of oil to heat a medium-sized house for a year. It takes 50,000 litres of aviation fuel to fly a jumbo jet from London to New York.

- If we go on using oil at the present rate, the known reserves of oil will last only 85 years.

- 88 out of every 100 barrels of crude oil are used to produce energy. 30 are used for cars and lorries, 23 to keep us warm, 15 in factories, 11 to make electricity and 9 to fuel ships, planes and trains. 7 go to make chemicals, and the rest are used in other ways: for road surfaces, for lubrication, for wax candles and even in greaseproof paper.

- Crude oil comes in a range of colours, from light and yellow (like cooking oil), to thick and black (like treacle). Crude oil still costs the same today as it did 100 years ago, compared with other products.

- There is an oilfield in southern England. The Wytch Farm oilfield produces 90,000 barrels of oil a day. Much of our oil was formed 250 million years ago during the Triassic period. In those days, the area around the Wytch Farm oilfield looked like Death Valley.

Paper

The Chinese made the first paper 2,000 years ago. They watched the way wasps used the chewed pulp from bamboo shoots to make their nests. In imitation, they then crushed bamboo shoots and made paper from the woody fibres.

The way we make paper today is still very much the same. We take wood and break it into tiny pieces. We boil it with water to make a pulp. We add dyes and chemicals to it. When the pulp is rolled, dried and cut, it becomes thin sheets of paper. It's a made material.

Glass

Natural glass materials are found in volcanoes. Silica sand is one of the Earth's most abundant minerals. Every sandy beach in the world has been made by water pounding rocks into sand – the major source of silica. Silica is turned by great heat into a natural glass called obsidian. The materials are fused together. Tremendous heat is required to melt silica, but soda compounds reduce its melting point and make it possible to melt it with less heat. When glass cools, it doesn't return to the crystal state of silica, but becomes transparent, rather like a frozen liquid. Glass sheets are rolled out to make windows. Originally, the silvered backs of mirrors were literally coated with silver. Nowadays a less expensive material is used. It turns a sheet of glass into a mirror.

Wood

Wood has many properties that make it useful. It is strong, quite easy to cut and shape, bendy and springy. It can be painted or varnished to look good. Most woods float on water, and wood absorbs water quite slowly. Wood is renewable or sustainable – if you plant more trees, you will get more wood.

There are two sorts of wood – hardwood and softwood – although these names aren't used to describe how hard the wood is. Softwoods are often lighter in colour – cream or yellow. Hardwoods are often darker brown. Softwoods have a wider grain; hardwoods have a closer grain. Balsa is a hardwood, as are lime and pear. Pine woods are softwoods.

Wood is used to make houses and furniture. Its ease of shaping and aesthetic qualities make it the ideal choice for things that look good, such as bowls and salad servers, and are pleasant to use.

Chips and boards

These days, children are more likely to come across wood products than natural wood. The table below shows some of the common wood products and their uses.

Wood product	How it's made	Where it's found
Chipboard	Scraps of wood waste glued and pressed together.	Planks and boards. Used for covering floors, and boarding lofts.
Fibreboard	Minced wood waste pressed together and baked to make a soft biscuit.	This is the pinboard material common in schools. Hardboard is a kind of fibreboard – used for cupboard backs.
Plywood	Many thin sheets of wood, cross-grained and glued together to make a strong board.	Strong material for light door panels, fascia boards, and outside use. Marine ply is used for boat-building.
Blockboard	Blocks and strips of wood sandwiched between thin wood boards.	Doors and work surfaces.
Veneer	A thin skin of high quality wood, covering poorer wood beneath.	Many examples in furniture, where cheaper wood is given an attractive finish. Also in more traditional car interiors.

Artifical materials

Plastic

'Plastic' is a word meaning bendy or supple. 'Plastikos' is a Greek word meaning mould or form. Many materials are 'plastic', such as clay or wax. But we commonly use the word to mean a group of materials that are manufactured from oil. The recent discovery of ways to change the chemical structure of oils has led to the petro-chemical industry and the development of plastics. About a tenth of thick black crude oil has the complicated chemicals in it that can be changed to plastic. After treatment, the gases and liquids from the crude oil become hard, shiny granules. This is plastic. Plastic can be coloured, melted, shaped, squashed, stretched, rolled into sheets or pulled into fibres. There are many different plastics, including:

- **acrylic**: hard, often clear. You can make spectacle lenses and telephones from acrylic

- **polystyrene**: hard and rigid. Polystyrene can be made into food containers and model kits. It can be cut,

glued and painted, but it breaks easily. 'Expanded' polystyrene is a light, soft material that reflects back the heat of your hand – it feels warm. It is used to pack delicate things and to line cool boxes

- **polythene**: light, tough and bendy. Made into buckets, bowls, bags and sacks. It takes forty years to decay, making it a good long-term insulation for electrical wires

- **PVC**: polyvinyl chloride is waterproof and a good insulator. It is used to make bags, luggage, coats, wellingtons and bouncy castles!

- **nylon**: a strong, light plastic that is great for fibres. Nylon fibres can make delicate stockings or tough bullet-proof vests. 'Crimped' or folded, nylon makes a bulky fabric that can trap air and keep you warm

- **PET**: polyethylene terephthalate is used to make plastic bottles, but Daimler-Chrysler believes it could make car bodies as crash resistant as steel, at half the price! Stand by for the plastic car!

- **PTFE**: polytetrafluoroethylene is used to make non-stick coatings on pans. PTFE is so slippery that it takes sandblasting and baking to make it stick to the pan! Its commercial name is Teflon.

Metals

Metals are so important to us that we have even named the biggest chunks of our history after the metal in widest use – the Copper Age, Bronze Age and Iron Age. We don't know how the first metals were discovered – very, very few are around in their pure state – but we might imagine that a stone-age family were sitting around the campfire made from a ring of stones. Suddenly one of them jumps to their feet. 'Hey, folks!' they say in the language of the time. 'Look at this shiny runny stuff coming out of these stones.' They don't touch it – it's very hot – but they notice the curious fact that when it has cooled, it has formed the shape it ran into. Now it's very hard, and cold to the touch, and it makes a strange ringing sound when you hit it. It might have cooled with a handy sharp edge. 'Hey, guys!' says our stone-age-soon-to-be-copper-age person. 'I've got a neat idea.'

Metals are great conductors – of heat, electricity and sound. In the temperatures on Earth, most familiar metals are hard. They reflect light well. They can be shaped into sheets and wires.

For scientists, metals include materials such as sodium and calcium that you wouldn't choose to make a bicycle from. There are precious metals like gold and silver; heavy metals like iron and lead; rare heavy metals like chromium and cobalt; light metals like aluminium and magnesium; and then the unexpected metals like sodium, barium and strontium.

Pure metals

Copper must have been an amazing advance over stone for tools and sharp edges for our early ancestors. Here was a material that was durable, pliable and resistant to corrosion (although it does collect a nasty green – and poisonous – verdigris on the outside, especially in damp conditions like modern bathrooms and kitchens). It also conducted heat easily and is an excellent conductor of electricity (as the first discoverers' descendants found out 500 years later). In fact, that is how it is most commonly used today – as electric wire.

Fascinating facts

- Every 24 hours, 25,000 hairs grow up to half a millimetre on the face of the average man. It takes a steel edge to remove them. The edge of a razor-blade can be one molecule thick. The modern safety razor was patented by King Camp Gillette and an engineer named William Nickerson, in 1901.

Hard, silvery-grey, easily shaped and pulled into wire, **iron** is a hugely abundant material and is responsible for a lot of colour in the world. From the red of our blood to the colour of bricks, iron and its products add colour to our surroundings. Only aluminium is a more common metal. Iron makes a good permanent magnet. It's perfect for electromagnets too. Solid and heavy, it's great for garden furniture, though you need to paint it or it oxidises (rusts).

Mercury is a heavy, silvery-grey liquid that is both poisonous and fascinating to explore. It can be found as a pure metal, but is more often mined as cinnabar ore.

But, which metal is the third most abundant element in the Earth's crust? Which metal was once so rare that Louis Napoleon, Emperor of France chose it for his cutlery rather than gold? Which metal is one third the weight of steel? Which metal has a natural coating that resists corrosion? Which metal is used for four out of five drink cans, worldwide? Most important of all, which metal could be 100 per cent recycled, saving up to 95 per cent of the energy needed to extract it from the Earth? Which metal is currently 63 per cent recycled in the UK?

The answer is **aluminium**. This metal is a rock product that surrounds us every day.

Alloys

'Wait a minute,' I hear you cry. 'If copper, iron, mercury and aluminium are natural metals, why have you put this section on metals under the heading 'Artifical materials'?' Well, I've put it here because **most** of the metals we use are mixtures of two or more metals – alloys – and they didn't mix together by themselves!

Our ancestors found that copper was too bendy to make a really good tool or weapon, so they found that the addition of another metal made it harder – with zinc it became **brass** and with tin it became **bronze** (harder and corrosion-resistant).

Perhaps our copper-age people discovered this for themselves and jumped into the Bronze Age, or possibly the first bronze they cast in their moulds was copper accidentally contaminated with tin.

Adding a tiny amount of carbon to iron makes **steel**, widely used for cars, ships and in building.

Increasing amounts of other metals make the so-called alloy steels like **stainless steel** – a steel with more than a tenth part of chromium in it. Stainless steel corrodes slowly.

A little chromium and nickel make a steel that is stainless, that is very strong and that resists rusting. Strangely, it is also non-magnetic. Because steel itself (and the iron from which it is made) is magnetic.

So which material is it?

If asked whether a particular material is a metal, children may lift the object to their cheek. Does it feel cold? Metals feel cold – so perhaps it's a metal. However, few materials match every criterion of a metal, a plastic or even glass. The next two pages will help you to classify materials, but to every rule there is an exception!

Is it metal?

Metals are:

- hard
- cold

Metals:
- expand
- bend
- stretch
- conduct electricity
- ring when you strike them
- feel heavy

Is it glass?

Glass is a hard material made from sand and soda. It:
- breaks easily into sharp-edged pieces
- lets light pass through it
- melts at very high temperatures

When heated, it can be:
- pulled
- blown
- shaped
- stuck to itself and to other materials
- moulded

Liquid glass can also have materials added that change its colour and strength.

Is it plastic?

Plastics are:
- light
- hard-wearing (durable)
- inexpensive

Plastics:
- don't rot
- don't dissolve in water
- don't conduct electricity
- can be made in many colours and shapes
- stretch, when they stretch, more in one way than another

They may be soft, bendy, hard, fragile, strong, or weak. You can make them so that they can be shaped when you heat them.

Is it wood?

Wood is a natural material. It is:
- strong
- bendy
- made of fibres

Wood:
- splits one way rather than another
- is harder to cut one way than another
- burns to leave a carbon ash
- usually floats
- can absorb water
- can be sanded smooth
- can be light or heavy

Is it paper?

Paper is a material made from wood fibres.
It can be:
- soft
- absorbent
- smooth
- white or coloured
- thin or thick
- folded and rolled
- burned to produce ash

Paper:
- takes ink and paint on its surface
- usually tears one way more easily than another
- is stiffer in one direction than in another
- resists compression better in one direction than another
- resists pulling better in one direction than another
- is broken up by water into fibres

Is it rock?

Rock is a natural material. It is usually:
- hard
- heavy
- smooth
- solid

It usually:
- resists striking
- can't be compressed or squashed
- can be polished to give a smooth surface
- can be split
- can be cut or sawn

It sometimes dissolves in water.

Safety and materials

At Key Stage 2, children should 'recognise that there are hazards in … materials … and assess risks and take action to reduce risks to themselves and others'.

Here are some questions you can ask children to highlight the potential dangers of working with materials. There is no need to cause alarm, but a little forethought will keep everyone safe.

- **Why are eating and drinking dangerous in science lessons?**

  There is an exception here. Lots of primary science involves eating! It is safe when children eat under your instruction and when the activity involves safe, non-allergenic food in hygienic conditions.

- **What happens next when testing forces?**

  This is always a good question to ask when testing a material to destruction. Has the next step been thought out? What happens when the elastic snaps, the bag breaks or the string unravels?

Fascinating facts

- Cereal crops like wheat and barley grew on long stalks for thousands of years. Scientists have now found a way of growing crops with a much shorter stalk so that more of the energy of the plant goes into making the edible seeds. Special long-stalked wheat has to be grown for thatching.

- The Romans used wood for their earliest forts such as Lunt Fort in Coventry, which has recently been restored and rebuilt.

- **What happens next when using hot water?**

  Pouring very hot water into a container not made for the job can result in the collapse of the container and a serious scald. There should be no need to use water any hotter than from the classroom tap.

- **What are the dangers of low and high temperatures?**

  While the dangers of high temperatures are well known, few children know that ice can burn. What should be done about a burn from a fire or something else hot? Children should know to put the affected part of the body in cold water and keep it there as long as possible. Taking the heat out of a burn this way prevents permanent damage.

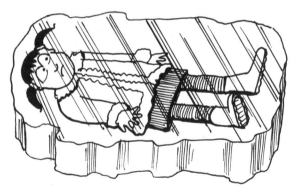

- **Can you make some safety rules?**

  Ask the children to think about avoiding accidents and risks, and also what to do if an accident occurs. What is the procedure? Who is the school first-aider? What should the children do until they arrive?

The storage and use of materials

- Not all kitchen or garden chemicals are safe to use in schools. Bleaches, cleaners, washing powders and liquids, and fertilisers are often harmful. If in doubt, check with 'Be Safe!' (see below). Store chemicals safely, well away from food materials, and make sure the storage container is securely locked. Children may need to wear eye protection if there is any risk of chemicals splashing or spitting.

- It's not often that you'll need sources of heat, but if you do, you'll find that hot tap water, or possibly a night-light in a sand tray, will meet all your needs. If you use these or a stove or other kitchen cooker, ensure a high degree of adult supervision.

- There's almost always a plastic substitute for glassware, even for mirrors. Have a plan for dealing with broken glass (thermometers, for example) which is safe for children, cleaning staff, and yourself.

For further information, there is one unrivalled source. 'Be Safe!', a publication of the Association for Science Education, ISBN 0 86357 324 X. This document is available from the ASE, from the School Science Service, or from SSERC in Edinburgh. Many local education authorities hold stocks, and issue them to their schools. This document is regularly updated in the light of new advice and experience.

Practical safety advice can be obtained from:

- The Association for Science Education, College Lane, Hatfield, Herts. AL10 9AA Tel: 01707 267411

- CLEAPSS School Science Service, Brunel University, Uxbridge UB8 3PH Tel: 01895 251496

- SSERC, 24, Bernard Terrace, Edinburgh EH8 9NX Tel: 0131 668 4421

Fascinating facts

- Aluminium is the commonest metal in the world. It is part of almost every rock. Gold is one of the rarest metals, which is one reason why it is so expensive.

- There is an annual competition in Derbyshire to make a woollen suit from sheep's wool in a day. The contestants take the raw sheep's wool and spin, weave, dye, cut and sew it to make a new suit.

Useful resources

Every school contains, and is made from, a wealth of different materials. Good starters for older children are the different types of **paper** in the school. Collect them, name them, talk about why each is different.

Encourage younger children to look at and label the **building materials** around the classroom and school. You can also buy materials kits. These have the advantage of doubtful materials being labelled. The disadvantages are that they are expensive and give you some very long names – polystyrene, for example. A set of stamped metals, however, can be helpful for this work, and for magnetism, too.

A set of **rocks** can be attractive, and you can use it for work on observation of differences. A set of **woods** will show different floating characteristics, as well as demonstrating that not all woods are the same.

You might think that **fabrics** would be easy. The complication is that fabrics from the ragbag are hard to identify and are almost always mixtures, meaning that it is difficult for children to classify them. Therefore, it can be worth buying a pack of labelled fabrics, too.

Activities

Level One

Choose ten different objects with care to create a varied sorting exercise. Aim for a range of materials, shapes and colours. Ask the children to sort the objects into three groups or sets. Provide three hoops for them to separate the sets. Encourage them to sort and resort in as many ways as possible. They could sort by colour, texture, shape and feel (cold or warm to the touch). They could sort by use or function.

Discuss the origins of the materials. Where did they come from? How were they made?

Level Two

Give the children some small desk drawer objects to sort. Encourage the children to pair any objects that have similar properties. This activity offers opportunities for looking at different sorts and uses of the same material. Aim for a wider range of materials than you provide at level 1. Introduce the idea of natural and artificial but note the cautions in the chapter.

Use two overlapping hoops to make a Venn diagram for sorting. For example, you could sort objects into metals and plastics but a pair of metal scissors with plastic handles belongs in both hoops.

Level Three

Give the children a collection of small objects, some made of iron or steel, and a magnet. Include a range of cans, showing that different materials are used for different types of can. Children may think that all metals are magnetic, so include some aluminium, copper or brass items, which are not. Ask the children to sort the materials into magnetic and non-magnetic.

Look for practical applications of this. Why do large cafés use steel cutlery? (They can separate it from plates and cups with a magnet.) How can a magnet be used to separate aluminium and steel cans? You could arrange a classroom can collection, recycle the cans and make both an energy saving and money for the school.

Level Four

Provide a range of building materials – bricks, tiles, slates – and ask the children to classify them and explain their classification in terms of what the materials do – for example, they make a strong structure, keep out the rain and so on. Encourage the children to think about the materials' properties and uses.

Survey a safe street with careful supervision. Look at the range of building materials. Ask each child to choose a building and record the materials used in its construction. (Do not take photographs of a house, shop or other building without the owner's permission.) Where are plastics used? (Gutters, pipes, door and window frames, fascia boards.) Why is this? (Rot and maintenance free.)

Level Five

Ask the children to complete a table listing characteristics of materials – magnetic, electrical conductor, thermal insulator and so on. Encourage them to include a wide range of materials in their tables.

Challenge the children to find some really unusual uses of materials. For example, the space shuttle 'Challenger' uses ceramic tiles on its outside to resist the tremendous heat of re-entry to the atmosphere.

Why are windows made from glass?

Now we all know the answer to that one, don't we? Windows have to be looked through and let light in. A fireguard must be made from a material that won't melt. A bicycle must be made from a material that is both strong and light. We always use materials that are best for the job.

Imagine a chocolate teapot or a paper bicycle. Chocolate and paper are both useful materials. But paper is good for writing on or for wrapping presents. Chocolate is good for eating. You need the right material for the job.

Best for the job

Suited to a task

Materials are chosen to suit a task. It is no good mending a roof with a permeable material, or filling window frames with something opaque. We select materials with great care, for a range of important qualities. Modern methods make it possible to design materials to suit tasks; for example particular qualities are built into plastics to suit the use to which they will be put.

Many materials are inherently strong. They may resist pushing forces, pulling forces, or even twist. Some resist all three. An iron bar is hard to stretch, but it's also hard to squeeze, and resists twisting forces, too. Some materials are strong only in one way, but that way is vital to their use. A rope resists pulling forces, but it would be

hopeless to use it as a chair – it wouldn't be able to resist the compression forces when you sat down.

We can add strength to materials in different ways. We can shape materials so that they are given strength by the way they are made. Disposable cups, for example, are made from thin, pliable plastic. If you cut the top edge from a plastic cup with a pair of scissors, you will find that the rim not only finishes the cup with a neat rim, but also resists squeezing.

Some plastic cups have a corrugation part way down the side – this provides a useful handgrip but it also adds strength. Plastic boxes, such as icecream containers, have both a rim and 'webs' in the plastic to add strength.

Some materials are deliberately made to be weak. The fastenings of food containers and the tabs on drink cans, for example, are intended to be opened easily. Folding, perforating, and scoring can weaken a material.

It's seldom obvious that the materials around us have been chosen for their properties, but it may be that characteristics of strength, hardness or flexibility have dictated their use. If natural materials with these qualities are not available, they can be manufactured by subjecting raw materials to physical or chemical change.

The behaviour of some materials may also come as a surprise. The fact that a paper boat may become waterlogged and sink, or that a structure made from the wrong materials may collapse, has to be learned by hard experience. We can, however, offer children opportunities to explore the range and uses of materials so they can investigate these surprising facts further.

Using paper – a great material

Paper is a good example of a material that is everywhere but has a great variety of special properties and uses. Before paper was invented, people wrote on bone, tablets of clay or strips of reed pressed together to make papyrus.

Today, we use paper for writing and printing, for wrapping and covering, when we go to the toilet and when we have a cold.

Paper is weak and strong

Paper tears easily. You might think it was very weak, but paper resists pulling well. We have to perforate it with tiny holes if we want to pull sheets off a roll. Paper resists squashing if it is folded or rolled. A tube of paper will hold quite a load.

Paper can be recycled. Used papers are collected and pulped again and the old fibres are made into new paper. Half of Britain's fibre for paper-making comes from waste paper, but we still throw away paper equal to the wood pulp from 50 million trees every year. However, wood pulp is renewable. If we plant trees as we cut them down then, in time, we shall have new trees for paper-making.

Metals – cold materials

In chemistry, the meaning of the word 'metal' is very different from the everyday one. For primary scientists, metals are cold, hard, shiny materials. Most are obtained by extraction from ores, but a few, largely precious metals are found in their pure state. This quality of remaining pure – of not reacting easily with the materials around them – is what makes them so lustrous and attractive. Their rarity ensures their value.

There are a couple of common confusions about metals. First, it is important to remember that not all metals are magnetic. The magnetic metals are iron, steel, cobalt and nickel, plus alloys of these.

Second, some metal objects are misnamed. A food 'tin', for example, is commonly made from steel. The surface is coated with tin to prevent rusting and contamination of the food. That is, unless the 'tin' is made from aluminium, like many soft drink cans. Even then, the lid may be made from tinned steel. Steel nails and wire are coated in zinc (galvanised) to resist corrosion.

Why that metal?

Task	Metal	Reason for choice
Building aeroplanes	Aluminium	Light weight and strength
Pots and pans	Copper	Good heat conducting qualities
Jewellery	Gold	Lustrous and corrosion-free
Chains	Iron	Strong, cheap, heavy
Weights	Lead	Heavy
Car wheels	Magnesium	Light weight, good-looking
Backing on mirrors	Silver	Reflective and fairly corrosion-free
Covering food cans	Tin	Corrosion-resistant
Covering steel	Zinc	Corrosion-resistant

Alloys

We often mix metals. We may blend them together to make an alloy. Alloys may be blended to give special qualities – strength, hardness or resistance to corrosion.

Task	Alloy	Reason for choice
Door knobs	Brass	Shiny surface
Bells	Bronze	Clear tone when struck
Taps	Gunmetal	Light and strong
Beer mugs	Pewter	Light and corrosion-resistant
Sealing metal joints	Solder	Melts at low temperatures
Strengthening concrete	Steel	Strong and flexible
Knives and forks	Stainless steel	Shiny surface, easy to clean, corrosion-free

Designer materials

An extraordinary revolution has overtaken the metal manufacturing industry (and other materials producers) in recent years. Materials can now be made that we know, before we start, will have certain properties. Scientists can make designer alloys. They decide what the metal should do, and then they make a metal that does just that. They may want a metal that is light, shiny, very strong, non-magnetic and must not rust. They can blend metals that have all these qualities, and make the alloy that is right for the job. These kinds of designer materials can be found in the houses we live in and the cars we drive. They are all around us.

Using clay

Most materials that we use have been changed in some way. Clay is dug from the ground. It is natural and easy to shape. It can be squeezed and shaped as it spins on a potter's wheel.

When water is added to it, the sloppy clay, called slip, can be put into moulds. When the clay has dried, it keeps the shape it had when it was wet. But if water is added to the dry clay, it will go soft again. This is a physical change and it can be reversed.

To change clay permanently, to make a chemical change, the clay must be heated in a hot oven called a kiln. It becomes a different material. If water is added, you will not get the clay back. The clay has become pottery. It has been chemically changed and this change is irreversible.

Using glass

Glass is a material that has been irreversibly changed. It is an extraordinary material – it is easily shattered, and yet it is one of the strongest materials known. It takes great heat to make glass. The change is chemical – and irreversible.

Glass is expensive to make. The natural materials it is made from are cheap, but the energy to make them very hot is expensive. Glass can be cleaned and reused. Glass from bottle banks is washed, sorted and put back into the glass-making process. This is not cheap either – glass has to be transported to the bottle factory, to the filling factory and finally back to the shops. But it saves on the energy that is needed to make new glass.

Examples of uses of glass are: windows, drinking glasses, all kinds of scientific instruments and containers, lenses, light bulbs and the fibres that transmit messages through cables.

Taking it lying down

Modern baths are mostly made from plastic, replacing the cast-iron bath and the zinc bath. They are made from thermosetting plastic – plastic that retains its shape once set. Glass fibre may be added for strength, and the moulded bath given reinforcement and support.

But just look at all the other materials that are used to provide you with a bathroom!

Object	Material	Origins
Lavatory bowl or washbasin	Porcelain	Clay
Bath or shower tray	Plastic	Oil
Tiles	Clay	Clay
Shampoo bottle	Plastic	Oil
Bath-salts jar	Glass	Sand
Taps, handles	Metal	Metal ores
Window and mirror	Glass	Sand
Toothpaste	Chalk	Limestone
Wall covering	Plaster	Gypsum
Pumice stone	Pumice	Volcanic lava
Talcum powder	Talc	Soapstone

Using plastic

Oil is a natural material. It can be used to make many things. Plastic is made from oil. It is a synthetic material that has been chemically changed so that it looks nothing like oil. First, the oil product is heated and chemically changed into pellets of plastic. The pellets of plastic can be coloured. The plastic can be heated and squeezed, pressed or sucked into a shape. When it is cold, it stays in that shape.

Oil can also be made into synthetic fibres to make clothes. These synthetic fibres can be spun, woven, or knitted together.

But plastic is not new! Although we have found new ways of using it, the plastics industry has a long history.

Date	Plastic	Inventor or manufacturer
1862	Celluloid	Alexander Parkes
1867	Celluloid	John Wesley Hyatt
1897	Casein	Adolf Spittler
1909	Bakelite	Leo Baekeland
1930	Polystyrene	I.G. Farberindustrie
1938	Nylon	Wallace Carothers
1941	Polyurethane	I.G. Farberindustrie
1990	Biopol	ICI
1995	Tencel	Courtaulds

Parkes and Hyatt both discovered celluloid independently. Although they were both exactly the same, Parkes called his discovery 'Parkesine' but failed to make it a commercial success.

Same problem, different answers

There is a growing uniformity in the way materials are chosen and used. This was not always so. When transport was a problem, houses were built with the materials to hand. Tudor houses around Stratford-upon-Avon, once deep in the Forest of Arden, were built with timber frames. The walls were made with wattle and daub – interlaced rods, plastered with mud, clay and animal droppings. The roofs were thatched with field straw or reeds from the river. The houses reflected the availability of materials in the region at the time.

In Wales, roofs were once always slated. Where slate was not easily available, local clay was baked into tiles. Clay was also used to make bricks – a stiff, sticky earth hardened in the sun or kiln to a handy, manageable size and shape, that could be bonded together with mortar – lime, cement, sand and water.

How is a modern house made?

Modern houses have two skins. The outer is brick, and the inner is commonly made from breeze blocks – grey, powdery, lightweight bricks made from cinders, sand and cement. The two are linked by wire ties, and the cavity between them is often filled with foam or loose insulating material.

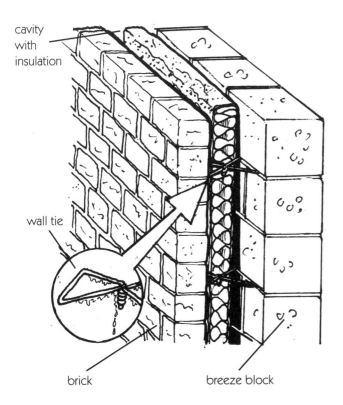

cavity with insulation

wall tie

brick

breeze block

- The addition of traces of lead to glass led to the clarity of crystal glass, and the use of glass for lenses. Modern uses of glass include optical fibres, used to carry light 'round corners' in the endoscope that enables doctors to see inside our bodies. Optical fibres can also be used to transmit a huge number of telephone messages simultaneously.

- Plastic bottles can be recycled to make fibres. These fibres can be turned into soft fleece material.

- The earliest form of celluloid was dangerously explosive. It was not unknown for celluloid billiard balls to be blown apart on impact.

- Nylon was first invented in 1938 and was one of the first synthetic fibres. It was used to make parachutes, as well as stockings and tights. There is a long-standing myth that it was named after New York and London. In fact, nylon was first called Fibre 66. Then it was called Norun, Nulon and Nilon, before the name Nylon.

The average three-bedroomed modern house is made from:

- 8,000 house bricks
- 2,250 breeze blocks
- 10 cubic metres of concrete
- 23 tonnes of sand
- 800 roof tiles
- 260 metres of roofing laths
- 4,500 litres of water
- 450 metres of electric cable
- 280 metres of copper piping.

Nowadays, these materials can be transported to the site. No wonder that in other times – and other countries – local materials were preferred.

Activities

Level One

If there is one material that a school contains in abundance and variety, it's paper. Invite the children to make a display of the paper in use in school. They can collect samples from the stock cupboard, library, kitchen and washrooms. The display will help children to consider the different uses to which we put paper. Ask the children to match paper type to use.

Ask the children to choose one type of paper and explain why it is used for a particular purpose – for example a paper towel is good for drying our hands because it is soft and absorbent.

Explore the different ways of joining paper: permanently as with glue and tape; and temporarily, as with paper-clips and staples.

Level Two

Tell the children to look at different materials around the classroom. Encourage them to relate the materials they see to their uses. Ask them why each material is used there. For example, wood is used for furniture. It is an ideal material for making furniture because it can be shaped and polished. It is strong and resists compressing and bending, plus it looks pleasing.

Why is metal used for pipes and taps? Why clay for cups and pipes? Why wood for pencils? Why plastic for 'tidy boxes'? Look for things that can be made from two different materials, for example rulers can be made from wood or plastic.

Level Three

Give the children some examples of materials and ask why these materials are especially suited to their use. For example, they could give reasons why glass is ideal for windows or copper for electric cables. They might then choose some examples of their own, such as the material they use for joining paper, and explain why it is suitable for the task.

Ask the children about the different ways of joining paper. Which are permanent and which are temporary? Which damage the paper? Invite the children to test how strong the joints made by various joining materials are.

For example, it takes a twisting force to break the joint created by an adhesive stick.

Level Four

Give the children a list of different purposes (for example, to prevent heat loss or to conduct an electric current) and challenge them to choose the best material for each one.

Ask the children to choose unsuitable materials for the job. Why is steel not a good material for covering cables? Why is cardboard not a good material for bicycles?

Level Five

Give the children a selection of materials and challenge them to distinguish the metals from the non-metals. What kind of tests can they use to identify the metals, other than examining their appearance (for example, seeing if they will conduct electricity)? Ask the children to identify, by name, as many of the materials as they can.

Collect plastics of different kinds. Most are labelled with their name – PTFE, nylon and so on. Notice that some materials can be manufactured in different forms, for example, nylon tights and nylon gearwheels. Relate the labelling to the recycling of plastic.

Keeping warm; keeping cold

We make judgements about how warm things are by comparing them with the temperature of our bodies. We feel a warm fire or a cold wind.

Sometimes, we make more precise judgements. Babies need to be bathed in water that isn't too hot. Parents sometimes test the bath water using their elbow. It's quite a good way to judge how warm the water is as the skin over your elbow has temperature sensors in it. All our skin has temperature sensors, but because there is little fat and muscle on your elbows, the skin there may be more sensitive.

Feeling warm on a cold day

If the sun is shining in through the windows, or the heating is on, you may be warm. If the windows and doors are open, and the heating is off, you may be feeling chilly. If you have a thick jumper on, you may be warm, even if the room is cold. Several factors determine how cold you may feel – how cold the room is, how warm your body is and how warm the radiators are. To know each of these factors, we have to compare temperatures with the temperature of our bodies. However, our bodies are not accurate measuring instruments.

You can see this for yourself by conducting the following short experiment. Fill three bowls with water. Fill one from the hot tap (not too hot!), one from the cold tap and one using half hot and half cold water. Put your bowls in a

row: hot, warm, cold. Put one hand in the hot water and one in the cold. Count to ten. Now put both hands in the warm water.

What do you notice? Because one hand has got used to hot water and the other to cold, they don't do a very good job of telling you how warm the warm water is. Why is using your body a poor way of measuring temperature? While a thermometer will give you an objective measure, based on a defined scale, your hands relate the temperature to previous experiences. The hand that has been in cold water senses the warm water as hot. The hand that has been in hotter water senses the warm water as cold. We have all had this sort of experience in the swimming pool, moving from toddler pool to main pool, from pool to hot shower. The sea, also, can feel very cold after you have been sitting on a warm beach.

Measuring temperature

Temperature is a measure of how hot something is, not how much heat there is in it. A bucket of hot water may have considerable heat in it, but it is not at the same high temperature as a light bulb or a sparkler firework.

Thermometers measure the level of heat in degrees. There have been several scales for measuring temperature, but the most common is the Celsius scale, named after Anders Celsius. This scale calls the freezing point of water 0°C, and the boiling point of water 100°C.

Fascinating facts

- Galileo was the first person to make an effective thermometer, in the year 1600. Galileo's 'thermoscope' used air, not water. It wasn't very accurate. For many years, liquid metal mercury was used in thermometers. But mercury is poisonous, so today alcohol is used instead. Alcohol is colourless, so it may be coloured blue or red so that you can see it.

Most thermometers measure this scale as well as measuring lower and higher temperatures. The Fahrenheit scale is still used in some countries and the Kelvin scale is used by scientists.

On the Celsius scale, the body temperature of a healthy human is 37°C. Sometimes, when you are unwell and have a slight fever, you can't control your body temperature well, and you may be hotter than this.

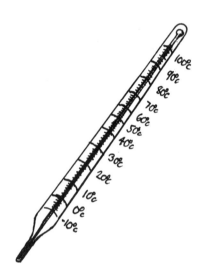

Using thermometers

If you are working with younger children, you may like to use the LCD descriptive thermometers that record the temperature either in relation to the human body ('colder than me') or the numeric ones that read temperatures in units of five degrees Celsius. These are unbreakable and quite accurate. You can stick them to the wall with sticky backed tabs or double-sided tape to find the warmest place in the room or the warmest room in the school.

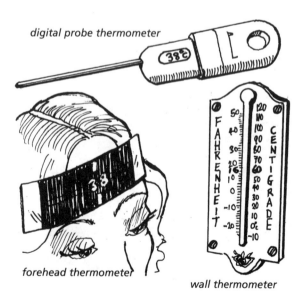

digital probe thermometer

forehead thermometer

wall thermometer

With older children, use liquid-filled thermometers (not mercury, of course), electronic digital thermometers or temperature sensors.

Thermometers and safety

Thermometers break very easily. Mercury ('silver') thermometers must not be used at home or at school. Mercury gives off a poisonous vapour. Glass thermometers, unless the 'caged' type, should have a plastic collar fitted which prevents them rolling off the table. You can wrap an elastic band round the end of the thermometer, which also works quite well.

Some thermometers work because special chemicals change colour at different temperatures. Other thermometers work because two different metals get bigger at different rates. A strip of these two metals stuck together, bends! Most thermometers work because liquids, like water, get bigger when they get hotter. You can see this by making your own thermometer. Fill an empty plastic drink bottle to the brim with water. Seal the top with modelling clay and push a straw through so that water starts moving up it. Even just putting your hands round the bottle will make the water expand and rise.

Thermometers have scales on them, like the scales on a ruler. As the liquid inside swells and shrinks, its top moves up and down the scale. You read the temperature by seeing where the top of the liquid is on the scale.

Temperature sensors

Temperature sensors work like a thermometer. If you plug a temperature sensor into a computer, the computer will record the temperature. It can keep records of changes in temperature over time.

Fascinating facts

● When you take an ordinary glass thermometer out of your mouth, the liquid begins to shrink. Your reading goes down. In 1866, a German scientist, August Kundt, invented a thermometer with a little kink in the tube. It reached body temperature very quickly. The kink stopped the liquid shrinking back. You have to shake the liquid back down before you can use the 'clinical thermometer' again.

So a temperature sensor will show you the changes as warm water cools down, or as ice melts. The computer software will recognise the temperature sensor when you plug it in. It will record the temperature in degrees Celsius.

Feeling the heat

A group of children set out to measure temperature changes in their school pond over one winter night. They left a sensor in the pond, planning to download their results the following day. The next morning was bitterly cold, and the sensor was frozen into the pond. When they had released it and downloaded the night's data, they found a moment, in the early hours of the morning, when the pond temperature dropped abruptly. At that moment, they reasoned, the pond had frozen over.

Temperature work like this offers excellent opportunities for using ICT in science. While thermometers can be used, temperature sensors can make it possible to watch temperature change taking place, to compare two temperature changes simultaneously and to record and print a graph of the changes.

Insulation

Heat is a form of energy that travels. It moves from hot places to cold. This is counter to common experience. We close doors 'to keep the heat in' or button up coats 'against the cold'. We can feel cold draughts. But heat actually moves out of a warm room, or is lost from a poorly insulated house. Objects left in a room will reach room temperature. Cold objects will gain heat from the room while hot ones will lose it. Eventually, both the objects and the room will reach the same temperature.

To slow the movement of heat, we use materials that are good thermal insulators. These reduce the speed with which heat moves. A hot water boiler that has been lagged with a 'tank jacket' will lose heat more slowly than one without. Similarly, a block of ice cream wrapped in newspaper will gain heat from the environment more slowly than an unwrapped one, and so will stay firmer for longer.

Good thermal insulators tend to be thick, loose-woven materials. This is because they trap air in their fibres. This air, being a poor thermal conductor, retains the heat. There are exceptions. Thin 'survival blankets' reflect body heat back, keeping you warm. They are insulators, but they are not acting in quite the same way.

Materials that are good thermal insulators do not conduct body heat away quickly. They may even feel warm to the touch, especially if they reflect our body heat back to us. Materials that are poor thermal insulators, but good thermal conductors, conduct our heat away from us very quickly and may feel cold to the touch. Your finger can freeze to an icy metal surface. Let's look at that again.

Room temperature

Everything in your bedroom that is not a heat source is at the same temperature. Yet curtains and door handles can feel as if they are at very different temperatures. Why?

You are warm. Your body is at a temperature of 37°C. When you touch something colder than you, heat moves from your body. It moves into the material you touch. If you touch a good thermal conductor, the material conducts heat away from you. It feels cold. If you touch a good thermal insulator, it is slow at conducting heat away from you. It feels warm to the touch.

Some materials, such as expanded polystyrene, may even reflect all your body heat back to you. You may think they are warmer than you. Curtains, carpets, clothes, blankets and duvets are poor thermal conductors. Door handles, metal hooks, metal hangers, windows and glass bottles are good thermal conductors and can feel cold.

White and light-coloured objects reflect heat while black and dark-coloured objects absorb it. Two cars in the staff carpark can be different in their internal temperatures – the black one may well be hotter inside than the white. You can feel the difference inside on a sunny day.

Why is your bedroom warm?

There are perhaps only two heat sources in your bedroom – a radiator or fire, and your body. To stay warm at night, the heat that both of these produce needs to be retained. We do this using materials called thermal insulators. Thermal insulators will vary with the home, but might look a bit like this:

Object	Material	Cause of warmth
Pyjamas, nightie, vest	Cotton, nylon	Trap heat with the warm air around body
Blankets, duvet	Wool, nylon, down	Trap heat with the warm air around body
Mat, carpet	Wool, nylon, other fibres	Insulate feet from the cold floor
Curtains	Cotton, other fibres	Keep the heat in the room
Window	Glass; wood or plastic frames	Keeps the heat in the room, especially if it is double-glazed
Walls	Brick, stone, breeze blocks	Keep the heat in the room, especially if cavity insulated
Ceiling and roof	Tile, slate	Keep the heat in the room
Loft insulation	Glass fibre	Thermal insulator; keeps the heat in the room
Cavity wall insulation	Glass fibre or polystyrene beads	Thermal insulator; keeps the heat in the room

Thermal insulators fall into three groups.

1   Those that trap air in their loose fibres and so retain your body heat – pyjamas, dressing-gowns, bedclothes.

2   Those, such as slippers and carpets, that keep you from direct contact with good thermal conductors, such as cold floors.

3   Those, such as curtains and loft insulation, that retain the heat in the room, from you, the radiator or the fire.

Air keeps in the heat

Pyjamas and double-glazing work in a similar way. By trapping air around you (which you warm with your body), clothes and bedclothes provide you with a cosy insulating blanket of air. By trapping air between the inside and outside panes, double-glazing makes use of this insulating property to keep the room warm.

Air is a remarkable insulator. It can work in some of the coldest places on Earth. Captain Scott led a team to the South Pole in the freezing Antarctic, but he was beaten there by a Norwegian explorer called Roald Amundsen. Amundsen's sledges were pulled by husky dogs. Why didn't the dogs freeze in the cold? The dogs had fur coats, which trapped the air and their body heat. In fact, the thick hairs of a husky dog's fur are also hollow. They actually have air inside them as well as between them.

Are you wasting heat?

Most homes in the country are wasting heat. People could be warmer and more comfortable, spend less money on fuel and help the environment by insulating their homes properly.

However, improving your home's insulation means spending money. Here are some of the changes you could make to your home. Next to each change is the cost of making this change to a three-bedroomed house.

Next is the amount you could save each year in fuel costs. Last of all is the time it will take for you to get your money back – the payback time. For example, you could spend £150 on draught-proofing your doors and windows. That would save you £25 a year on wasted heating fuel. In six years, you would have saved enough to pay for your draught-proofing. After that, you would be saving £25 every year at 2001 prices!

House improvement	Approx cost	Approx saving every year	Payback time
Loft insulation	£250	£125	2 years
Cavity wall insulation	£360	£240	1.5 years
Draught-proofing	£150	£25	6 years
Double-glazing	£6,000	£240	25 years
Better boiler controls	£240	£60	4 years
A new, better boiler	£1,200	£300	4 years

Double-glazing may not look like a bargain, but it is certainly the best way to replace rotting window frames. If you have no other effective form of insulation, double-glazed windows will reduce heat loss through the windows, which amounts to 25 per cent of the heat loss from a detached house.

In addition, lagging your hot water tank insulates it and keeps the hot water hot. Putting thermal insulation in the loft helps stop heat escaping. Injecting thermal insulation into wall cavities helps stop heat escaping.

References

These sites will give you background information – and help you with home insulation!

www.est.co.uk
The Energy Saving Trust offers good independent advice on energy conservation for householders and small businesses.

www.create.org.uk/
Everything you need to know about energy education.

www.rmi.org/sitepages/pid506.asp
Good ideas regarding energy conservation and product innovations.

www.defra.gov.uk/environment/index.htm
The government's website includes facts on energy consumption in the UK.

www.doingyourbit.org.uk
The latest campaign from the DEFRA (Department for Environment, Food and Rural Affairs) about doing your bit to help save the planet.

Activities

Level One

Ask the children to choose clothes for a sunny day and clothes for a cold day. Compare their choices and discuss why they are different. What is it about certain materials that makes them suited to a cold day? Encourage the children to avoid saying that they are 'warm'. They may feel warm to the touch, but their quality is that they keep in your body heat.

Ask the children to make a display, with labels, of their choice of clothes for cold days and warm days.

Level Two

Ask the children to suggest the best material for keeping things warm. Then let them experiment by using plastic bottles of warm water and putting different 'hats' and 'scarves' on them. Which material will keep the water warm for longest? Tell the children to measure the outcomes subjectively by feeling the bottles with their hands. They should feel them at intervals and record the changes.

Level Three

Ask the children how to keep a hot drink hot. Using water at a safe temperature, ask them to compare a range of plastic drink containers – for example, from fast food outlets, supermarkets and the school kitchen. The children should use thermometers to compare starting temperatures and temperatures after a standard time. Which container keeps the heat best? Why?

Using the same range of plastic drink containers, now ask the children to test their effectiveness in keeping things cold. Tell the children to use ice cubes in the cups, sealing them and opening them only when an ice cube melts. How much ice is left in the cup? Which is the best insulator? Are the results the same as for the hot water test?

Record the results on a graph. This could be a line graph but, for this level, a stick graph may be more appropriate. Then, at Level 4, the points can be joined to show that the cooling is continuous – a 'cooling curve'!

Level Four

Ask the children to record a cooling curve for one or more different thermal insulators. Tell them to put hot water in a cup with a lid – a fast food cup with a hole in the lid for the straw is ideal – and put a thermometer through this hole. They should record the starting temperature and then the temperature every five minutes. Ask them to plot their results on a graph and join the points to record a cooling curve.

Ask the children to compare the cooling curves of two or more cups. What story do they tell? Do the cups lose heat quickly or slowly? Ask them to explain their results and to compare them with everyday experiences – keeping drinks hot and wearing a hat on a cold day.

Level Five

Challenge the children to keep an ice cube, unmelted, for as long as possible. They can use any materials they like – within reason – but not the fridge. Ask them to record their results and explain them.

Set the children the challenge of keeping a drink hot for as long as possible. They can choose the materials they use, record and explain their results.

Solid, liquid or gas?

Water

Water is a familiar material which offers a wealth of opportunities for play and exploration. Children will have seen water in several different forms – liquid water, solid ice, gaseous steam. Water changes state easily, back and forth, from one form to another. Other materials do the same – wax and chocolate, for example. But only water easily offers all three states – solid, liquid and gas – in our everyday experience. And it's never possible to get the wax and chocolate back just the way they were!

Water is the liquid state of the material. Liquid water is essential for life. Liquid water takes the shape of the container you put it in, whether it be a bucket, cup or jug. It flows downhill, but it won't go up except in a flood (although you can make a continuous column of water flow over and down if you use a siphon). Children will have had a lot of experience of water and its qualities in the bath, swimming pool and water tray.

Ice

Ice is the solid form of water. It is formed when pure water drops in temperature below 0°C. An amazing quality of water is that it expands as it freezes – tops are pushed off milk bottles and car radiators can be cracked. Frozen water takes up more space than it did as a liquid. As a result, the ice is less dense than water – the same mass of water is now taking up more space – and it floats. If ice sank, it would be disastrous for water life. Plants and water animals would be crushed under it. It seems unlikely that life would ever have got started on Earth if ice sank.

Steam

Strictly speaking, the billowing clouds that come from a boiling kettle are water vapour. Steam itself – water in its gaseous state – is invisible. You can see where it is by looking carefully at the spout of a boiling kettle – you can just see a clear space between the spout and the vapour. (You will need to hold the switch of an automatic kettle on, otherwise it will turn itself off just as you are getting interested!) This invisible gas is true steam.

The stuff that fills the bathroom, making 'condensation' run down the cold mirror and windows, is water vapour – liquid water in tiny droplets. It condenses on cold surfaces. This process is called 'condensation', and the liquid that condenses is called 'condensed water'. However, if you tell your neighbours that you are having trouble with condensed water on your double-glazing, they may think you're a bit of a pedant.

Fascinating facts

- People lost in the desert have survived by drinking water that had evaporated and condensed. There is water in damp sand. If you dig a hole in the sand and cover it with a plastic sheet, the water will evaporate from the sand and condense on the sheet. A weight in the middle of the sheet makes the drips run to the middle. Put a cup there to collect the water.

Think about these materials: syrup, ice, the contents of an 'empty' bottle, modelling clay, aluminium foil, flour, sawdust and jelly. Decide whether each is a solid, a liquid or a gas. Think of some reasons for your decisions.

The syrup is a liquid. It may be slow to pour, but it does pour and it forms a flat top. The ice is solid. It has a shape and resists squashing. A bottle isn't 'empty' – it is full of gaseous air.

Modelling clay is a funny material – a solid that doesn't resist squashing much. Closer to a solid than a liquid, it nevertheless has liquid in it, and it is the mix of solid and liquid in modelling clay that makes the particles easily moveable. As they slide past each other, the clay changes shape.

Foil squashes easily – but there is no question that it is a solid. Flour actually pours – as do other powders. But it doesn't form a flat top – it may be made of tiny pieces, but it is a solid. So is sawdust.

Jelly is interesting. It is both solid and liquid – the solid forming a lattice, inside which are particles of liquid. Heating a jelly, or putting a cube in water, breaks down the solid lattice and releases the liquid. Other materials are made of mixtures like this.

Mixtures of materials

Some 'in-between' materials are mixtures of materials – a liquid in a gas, a solid in a gas, a liquid in a liquid, a solid in a liquid, or even a liquid in a solid.

Smoke is a solid (dust) in a gas (air). 'Steam' is a liquid (water vapour) in a gas (air) – but remember that true steam is water gas and is invisible. French dressing is liquid in liquid. The two liquids, oil and vinegar, don't stay one liquid for long, and quickly separate without an

emulsifier. Mayonnaise is liquid in liquid. Again, oil and vinegar do not mix, but adding egg yolk 'emulsifies' the two, keeping the oil in suspension. You use a lot more emulsions than you notice – not just in paint, but in many cosmetics, where oil is dispersed through water. Shaving foam is gas in liquid. The liquid soap foams because of the gas propellant.

What happens to the particles?

Solids keep their shape. They are hard to squash or compress. They may be found in sheets and bars, or even as powders. Metals are solids, but so are sawdust and flour. Sawdust and flour pour like liquids, but they make piles with a pointed top. The tiny particles that make up a solid are in fixed positions.

There are spaces between the particles and the particles vibrate.

Liquids pour. They take up the shape of whatever holds them – the cup, bottle, bowl or jug. But liquids have a flat top when you pour them into something. You would be very surprised if you ran a bath, only to find that it came to a point in the middle! Liquids are hard to squash or compress. Water is a liquid, as are milk, vinegar and oil. The tiny particles that make up a liquid move and flow.

There are spaces between the particles and the particles move, sliding around each other.

Fascinating facts

- Ooblek is the name given to a cornflour and water paste. Add some water to some cornflour. You will find that the paste has strange properties. It is somewhere between a solid (you can squeeze it into a ball) and a liquid (the ball will collapse and run through your fingers).

- Gases have weight. A blown-up balloon weighs more than a flat one. But some gases are less dense than air (including hydrogen and helium) and hot air is less dense than cold. So gas balloons and hot-air balloons rise.

- One of the qualities that makes chocolate so appealing is that it melts at a temperature close to body temperature. So it goes into your mouth as a solid and becomes a liquid on your tongue.

- Most liquids shrink to become solids, but water expands when it is frozen to ice.

Gases fill the space around them. Oxygen is a gas, as is carbon dioxide (the bubbles in fizzy drinks). The tiny particles in gases are free to move anywhere.

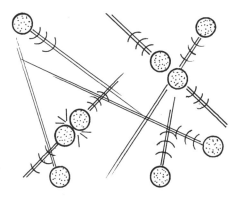

There are spaces between the particles. The particles are free to move, and they do!

Open a new air freshener, put it on a table and then walk around the room. How quickly does the smell fill the room? Where do you have to stand so that you cannot smell it? Everything is made up of tiny particles. They are closely packed in solids, freer to move in liquids and freest of all in gases. How does that explain your air freshener?

The solid material in the freshener is losing particles. The particles are floating off and arriving in your nose, an organ designed to accept the tiny particles in a gas. Although your nose isn't in direct contact with the air freshener, you know it is in the room!

Melting

When solids melt, they become liquids. They can flow and pour, and fill a shape. Some solids melt when they are heated. Butter melts to become a liquid. Chocolate melts, too. Both become solid again when they are cooled. Chocolate is not changed much by the melting. But the butter loses water when it melts. So the butter is changed by the melting. You can't change it back.

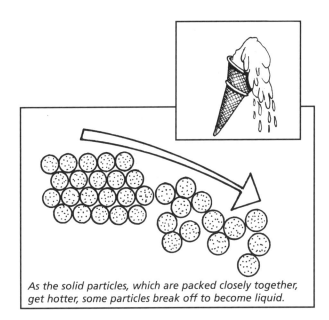

As the solid particles, which are packed closely together, get hotter, some particles break off to become liquid.

Metals melt to become liquids. We can use this to help us shape the metal. When the metal is hot and runny, the liquid metal can be poured into moulds. When the liquid metal cools, it takes the shape of the mould. For more on changes of state, see Chapter 7.

Activities

Level One

Encourage the children to experiment with liquids – pouring them, mixing them and comparing volumes and behaviour.

Give the children a range of plastic moulds and ask them to use them to make different ice shapes. Apart from ice cube trays, they might try plastic jelly moulds, lolly moulds, plastic beakers, and other small plastic containers. Point out that the ice shape matches the mould. Encourage the children to notice that the ice expands as it freezes. Water is unique in getting larger when frozen.

Level Two

Give the children a selection of materials and ask them to classify the materials into solids and liquids. In the selection include some complex materials, such as powders, salt and sugar, as well as easier examples. Give them some thicker liquids, too – toothpaste, honey and syrup, for example.

Ask the children how they identified the liquids. How can their 'runnyness' be compared? Ask the children to try trickling very small amounts down slopes. Which is the fastest or the slowest? How does this relate to their thickness? They could also try dropping clean marbles into jars of these liquids and noting which sinks fastest.

Level Three

Ask the children to identify gases around them, such as air, and carbon dioxide in soft drinks. Encourage them to experiment with the ways that gases spread in a room – by, for example, using smelly substances such as an aerosol air freshener.

Help the children to conduct some research on gases using books, the internet and CD-Roms. Subjects to include in the research project might include the uses of gases (balloons, as a fuel), the air and how it is made up, 'phlogiston' – once believed to be the burning part of air, and the discoveries of great scientists like Antoine Lavoisier.

Level Four

Give the children a bottle of fizzy drink. Ask them to identify the three states of matter – the solid bottle, the liquid drink and the gas in the drink.

Use water as an example of a material that we see existing in all three states. Compare and contrast the differences between water, ice and (teacher only) steam or water vapour. The latter, using a kettle, must be a demonstration only, for safety reasons. Take safety precautions to protect children from both the hot water and the mains electricity. Avoid trailing leads. Emphasise to the children that the clouds are water vapour, not steam. Steam is invisible – a gas. Collect the water vapour on a cold surface (fill a jam jar with ice, or bring it straight from the fridge).

Level Five

Ask the children to identify mixtures of solids, liquids and gases – for example, shaving foam (a gas in a liquid), or jelly (a liquid in a solid). Ask them to identify, by experimentation, some liquids that don't mix, such as cooking oil and water. They could use CD-Roms or the internet to find out more about the states of matter.

Push a pin through the centre of a drinking straw. Support the pin on both sides, between books, for example, so that it makes a light, delicate balance. (You can balance it by snipping bits off the ends of the straw.) Now try adding balloons to each end, both empty and full of air. Challenge the children to predict what will happen. A blown-up balloon will not lift the end in the air! It will pull it down – air has weight.

Can you make bread from toast?

Physical or chemical change?

The difference between physical and chemical change is that whereas physical change is only a change in form – the substance is still there – chemical change is when new and irreversible substances are created. Sugar dissolving in tea is a physical change, but baking a cake is a chemical change.

Some physical changes are irreversible. Try sawing your leg off to see what I mean. No chemical change has taken place but reattachment could be difficult.

So think of it this way:

Physical changes involve the rearrangement of particles – mixing, separating, putting them in a different state (solid, liquid, gas) or otherwise doing something to them without actually changing the particles themselves.

Chemical changes give you something new. The particles have been changed by splitting or combining with others, or by changing partners so that they produce a new material you didn't have before.

So making sawdust is a physical change (which is irreversible) but making ammonia from hydrogen and nitrogen is a chemical change which is reversible – you can get the hydrogen and nitrogen back.

So – although most physical changes are reversible and most chemical changes are not, there are exceptions!

Make a cup of tea. As you do so, explain to yourself what you are doing in scientific terms. Which changes taking place are physical? Which are chemical? Which are permanent? Which are reversible?

Now open a bottle of fizzy drink. Is there a physical change or a chemical one? Is something new being produced, or is it just a case of separation? Is there a gas being made, or is the gas just coming out of solution?

Toast some bread. What kind of change happens? Can you reverse it? What is the material that forms on the surface of the bread? Burned toast is carbon. That's a new material, so the change is a chemical one.

Does salt disappear in water?

If you ask children what happens when something dissolves, they will often tell you that it 'disappears'. This seems to be true of materials that dissolve to make a colourless liquid – like salt or sugar. But dissolving instant coffee produces a material where the coffee has far from disappeared – it is clearly there throughout the changed, coloured liquid.

Dissolving takes place when one substance is dispersed through another to become a single material. This material is called a solution. In theory, the substances involved could be solids, liquids or gases. In practice, children will come across this most often when they add something solid to a liquid – for example, salt to water or sugar to tea. (The solid and the liquid are called the **solute** and the **solvent**, but these are not essential terms at this level.)

When a solid dissolves, it becomes dispersed throughout the liquid. If you were to sample any part of the liquid, you would find the solid there. This is not what happens when you add something insoluble to liquid (when it lies at the bottom or floats on the top) or something that forms a suspension, like flour (where the bits float about until they sometimes sink to the bottom).

When a white or colourless solid is added to water, it appears to disappear. Tasting safe materials in solution proves that the solid is still there. Coloured solids may colour the water, and the children can see how they colour the whole of the solvent evenly.

Can't take any more!

When the solvent cannot dissolve any more of the solute – the water cannot dissolve any more salt, for example – then the solution is **saturated**. Again, this is not a word for primary children, though they will observe that salt will not go on dissolving in water forever. You can increase the amount of solute that the solvent will dissolve by raising the temperature of the solution, but as soon as the temperature falls, the solid comes out of solution again.

Raising the temperature of the solute and stirring are familiar ways of speeding up dissolving. These two methods work because both encourage the release of the tiny particles of solid into the liquid. As a child once said when explaining dissolving, 'If you dropped me in hot water and then hit me around the head with a spoon, I'd let go of my friends, too!'

Dissolving should not be confused with melting – the change of state from solid to liquid with increased temperature. However, some materials melt and dissolve simultaneously. Jelly can become a liquid and disperse through the water when stirred with hot water.

What really happens?

What happens to things that dissolve? Children's views may reflect their observations. Consider the following:

'When I add sugar to my tea, it just disappears. You see the same thing when you add salt to water; first it's there and then it's not. The water won't weigh any more with the salt in it – it's just disappeared. You could go on adding salt if you liked. It would just go on filling the spaces.'

Surely the salt has to go somewhere? When you add a solid that will dissolve, to a liquid, it begins by filling the spaces between the particles of liquid. Rather like a cinema with a fixed number of seats, the liquid will take so many arrivals before it is full. When it is full, the liquid can take no more, and is said to be saturated. The excess, like disappointed film-goers, is rejected and sinks to the bottom. Strangely, the level of the solute actually falls at first.

But some materials, like sand, don't dissolve. They may sink to the bottom of the liquid or, if they are low density, they may sit in mid-water or in suspension. If you put the liquid through a filter, only dissolved particles pass through. Large, undissolved particles are netted and stay behind. If you then let the water evaporate, you will be left with the dissolved solid, which may form crystals.

Changing state

The concept of materials changing is a difficult one. It's not surprising that children recognise changes when they are spectacular – a colour change, a flame, smoke – but not when they are unexciting.

They may feel that 'Stuff disappears.' There was a match, it was lit, and now it's gone. They may think that the product was somehow inside the original material – thus rust may be thought to ooze out of a corroding nail. They may simply think that one material has 'turned' into another – the flour and water have turned into bread – without a word of explanation.

Sometimes we need to bring the material back – only then can we show that it was there all along.

Separating materials

Undissolved solids can be separated from a liquid by filtering, a process that uses paper as a kind of sieve. So we can get sand back from water simply because water goes through the filter but sand does not.

Dissolved solids cannot be separated from the solution by filtering. They have to be reclaimed by evaporation. Evaporation is a process by which a liquid turns to a vapour without boiling. Even cold water loses vapour to the air because some of its molecules have the energy necessary to escape. Making the liquid warmer gives the molecules more energy. This means they can escape more easily, and so the liquid evaporates more quickly.

Many common materials, such as sugar and salt, have an orderly three-dimensional arrangement of their atoms or molecules, and this is reflected in their shape. A common salt molecule, for example, is a perfect cube; salt crystals are cubic. Materials like salt crystallise when the liquid they are dissolved in evaporates. Crystals often form round a 'seed' – a speck of dust or an existing crystal.

Condensation is a process by which a vapour or a gas turns back to a liquid. Water vapour condenses on a cold window, and collects in a liquid form again.

These are all reversible changes.

Cooking and change

Most cooking is an example of irreversible chemical change. The science involved is engaging. First, there are the ingredients – the solids, liquids and in-betweens – that can be mixed, rubbed or creamed. Just combining ingredients changes them irreversibly. Heating changes them in chemical ways and results in completely new products.

Toast is different from bread. You can't get the bread back again. That's not true of adding materials to water. You can get the salt back again from brine, and taste the sugar in a fizzy drink.

There is science in simple meals like Welsh rarebit. Toasting the bread drives off the moisture and turns some of the surface to carbon – too much if you burn it!

Buttering the hot toast melts the butter. Water is lost and the butter is permanently changed. Cheese is changed by heating, too. It becomes rubbery and stringy. Its flavour is different, and can be enhanced with a sprinkling of pepper. Compare a hot cheese toastie with the raw ingredients and see the differences.

Cooking vegetables changes them in three ways. First, it softens them, breaking down the structure. Adding bicarbonate of soda speeds up this breakdown and keeps the colour of green vegetables, but it also destroys their vitamin C. Second, starch bursts out of many vegetables. Mashed potato, for example, becomes a jelly-like mass. Third, coloured materials come out of vegetables such as cabbage or beetroot, colouring the water.

Following a recipe should result in the same product every time, but cooking is a mysterious mix of science and art, and even with the best precautions, cakes can fail to rise, pizzas burn and bread comes out of the oven underdone. But even disasters can be educational. Usually too much interference with the process, rather than too little, results in a peculiar looking dish. You can usually eat it, anyway!

The chemistry of a cake

Most cakes contain flour, sugar, eggs and butter, perhaps with some baking-powder. All these are changed in the processes of beating, folding and baking and the change is permanent. At each stage, you can see changes. The ingredients may change colour, or consistency, or they may work together to make something new!

You might start with a block of butter and some caster sugar. The butter is a combination of solid fat and water.

Beating it together with the sugar helps the butter spread evenly through the mixture. The butter is important. Like it or not, fat adds taste to food. Beating also traps air bubbles in the mixture. The bubbles will be important later. This mixture is lighter in colour than the butter.

Then you beat eggs into the mixture. This traps more air, and the sugar dissolves in the water from the eggs. The mixture has changed. It has become a colloid – it is made up of tiny particles of one material (the sugar) dispersed through another (the butter and eggs).

Folding the flour and baking-powder in gently keeps the air bubbles in the mixture, and spreads the flour and baking-powder particles through the mixture. They hang in the mixture as a suspension.

Cooking the cake

Now you are ready to cook. A greased baking tin should stop the mixture sticking. A pre-heated oven helps, too. In the twenty minutes or so that the cake is in the oven, every ingredient will be changed.

The butter will melt and then solidify as the cake cools. But it will be permanently changed. It loses its water and the water vapour from the butter makes bubbles, lightening the cake. The flour chemically changes. The cooked flour is stiffer than the raw flour, making the cake firmer. The eggs will also have changed, adding to the firmness of the cake. The sugar will give the new cake its sweet taste. Sugar on the outside of the cake will have caramelised, giving the cake its brown colour.

The baking-powder will have reacted with itself. Baking-powder, the invention of the same Mr Bird who gave us custard without eggs, contains bicarbonate of soda and a mild acid – sometimes cream of tartar. Alfred Bird invented it during the Crimean War so that soldiers at the front could have risen bread without yeast. Bicarbonate of soda reacts with an acid (you will have seen it fizz with vinegar) to make carbon dioxide gas. The carbon dioxide bubbles make the cake light in texture. This is yet another chemical change!

Safety when cooking

- Children must wash carefully and wear aprons or overalls. Hair must be tied back.

- Containers and tools should be used strictly for cooking only.

- Surfaces must be cleaned down with mild disinfectant before use.

When a candle burns

There are irreversible changes that we see frequently in primary science but that are still hard to explain. Take, for example, the burning of a candle. We can all recognise the stages – solid, liquid, gas – that the wax goes through as the candle burns. But where has the 'lost' wax gone? The fact is that the products of burning wax (water vapour and carbon dioxide) are lost invisibly. So the change that children observe is the gradual shrinkage of the candle. It doesn't seem logical, but remember that we often fill the petrol tank of the car, and don't expect to clear out a load of ash next time we stop for fuel.

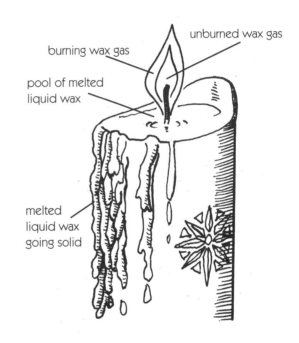

burning wax gas

unburned wax gas

pool of melted liquid wax

melted liquid wax going solid

Fascinating facts

- We value materials that resist change. Gold is very reluctant to combine with other materials and so it keeps its sheen when steel would rust or copper turn green. But even gold can tarnish in time and a golden dome in the Polish city of Krakow has been encased in plastic to protect it from pollution.

- Some forms of carbon are resistant to change. Carbon fibre is a black, silky material made from pure carbon. Courtelle acrylic carbon fibre has four times the strength of steel and glows in flames without changing.

- Diamond is the hard, crystalline form of carbon. It is the hardest substance known. It takes a temperature of 3,000°C to make a synthetic diamond.

Activities

Level One

Invite the children to dissolve different materials in water and observe the outcomes. They could use sugar, salt, instant coffee and sand, for example. Does sand dissolve? What other materials do not dissolve in water?

Together, look at the list of ingredients needed for a cake. Ask the children about the way the various ingredients are combined and baked. Compare, if possible, a finished cake with the ingredients.

Level Two

Help the children to explore the fact that liquids dissolve in liquids. For example, ask them to make up some fruit squash. Explore further examples of dissolving. Ask the children whether they can get the dissolved materials back. Tell them to leave their samples to 'dry out' and see.

Clay modelling will show the children how materials change. Air drying a clay model will turn it to a form that potters call 'leather', but is this a permanent change? If the children add water to their dried models they will find that they become wet clay again. Firing their pottery will produce permanent change. The kiln heat chemically changes the clay – it changes its nature completely. Its colour will change, and even the way it sounds when struck. Show the children that a fired pot holds water. It doesn't dissolve or even soften.

Level Three

Ask the children for their ideas about what increases the speed of dissolving. Then encourage them to test out their ideas. They could, for example, try using warm water, stirring with a spoon, or using more water, to compare the dissolving of salt in water. Remind them to control the factors involved – if they change the water temperature, for example, they should keep the water and salt quantities the same. What combination of factors will make the salt dissolve fastest?

Let the children use candle-making kits to experiment with melting and shaping candle wax. Light a candle and encourage the children to observe the liquid wax in the top of the candle, and imagine the gas in the blue and yellow of the flame. Encourage very careful observation. What happens after the candle is blown out? (There are few risks with candles, providing hair and

loose clothing are tied back, and children are instructed not to lean across the candles, or carry them about. Support candles with sticky backed tabs in a metal tray. Always light them yourself.)

Level Four

Ask the children to dissolve jelly in water. Remind them to control the different factors involved. Does the colour of the jelly make a difference? Different groups of children could change different factors. Which is the factor that really affects the speed of dissolving? Is this dissolving only? In fact, jelly cubes also melt. Demonstrate this to the children by melting one over warm water. Compare the speed of dissolving a jelly cube with the speed a jelly cube melts. Put one in warm water and the other in a plastic cup floating in the warm water.

Burn a candle and ask the children what is happening. What is burning and what changes are taking place? (The changes are far more apparent in a small cake candle, which burns down faster than a larger candle.) The wax near the wick melts, rises up the wick, and is burned as a vapour. The wick itself burns where it is outside the vapour, in the air. Ask about the candle. How has it changed? What has been used up? What, if anything, has stayed the same? Note that the melted wax that runs down the candle has changed, too.

Level Five

Challenge the children to find out how much salt can be dissolved in a quantity of water. What happens when the water becomes 'saturated', when it can take no more salt? Explore saturation. Does increasing the temperature of the water make it possible to dissolve more? Ask the children what happens as the solution cools.

Use the children's accumulated knowledge to tackle a challenge such as separating salt and sand. Add water to the salt and sand mixture and then ask the children to take the sand and the salt out of the solution. (While the sand can be filtered from the water, the salt will need evaporation to be recovered.)

Is soil made from dinosaur droppings?

We live on a rocky planet. Wherever we are, even in the middle of the ocean, there are rocks beneath our feet. These rocks were formed as the Earth began to cool.

That cooling process is far from over. Under the hard, cold crust of the Earth, the mantle and core of the planet are still intensely hot. They are so hot that molten rock periodically bursts through the crust as volcanoes.

Much of the rock on the Earth's surface was formed from this original material, the so-called igneous rocks. But some have been eroded, transported and laid down in layers of sediment (sedimentary rocks). Some of these have been subjected to intense heat and pressure and have changed or metamorphosed (metamorphic rocks).

We take these rocks and their products for granted – we use marble or granite for building and slate for roofs. These materials are all around us.

Rocks are constantly being broken down. The final product of this breakdown is soil or 'earth'. Unlike the child who guessed that earth was made of dinosaur droppings, we know that soil is a rich, complex material.

The study of rocks and soils at primary school is concerned with the recognition of rock types (slate, marble, chalk, granite, sand or clay), the different forms of rocks (pebbles, stones) and the characteristics of rocks and soils (their colour, texture, drainage and absorbency).

How to spot common rocks

Rock	Description
Black slate	Flat, metamorphic, black with carbon.
Quartzite	Metamorphic with very hard interlocking crystals.
Schist	Colourless, flaking metamorphic, easily breaks into layers.
Gneiss	Metamorphic rock with clear bands.
Marble	Metamorphic, white and smooth.
Feldspar porphyry	Large crystals of igneous feldspar in crystal.
White granite	Igneous, white crystals with flat surfaces.
Granite	Igneous, crystalline.
Gabbro	Igneous, interlocking light and dark crystals, half and half.
Basalt	Igneous, light and dark crystals.
Limestone	Crystalline; scratches easily.
Quartz sandstone	Sedimentary, sandy.
Breccia	Sedimentary, angular fragments.
Sandstone	Round red grains, sedimentary.

Lots of rocks

There is a wide variety of rocks. They have different characteristics. They vary in hardness, for example, and a scale of hardness, Mohs scale, is based on 'what scratches what'.

Here are some familiar rocks. They have different qualities and therefore different uses.

- **slate**: rock that splits into smooth plates – used for roofs and, in the past, for writing.
- **marble**: hard limestone, easy to polish – used for worktops and statuary.
- **chalk**: soft limestone – used for chalkboards.
- **granite**: hard rock full of crystals – used for building.
- **sand**: grains of rock – mixed with other materials to make concrete.
- **clay**: soft, sticky soil – baked to make a range of products.
- **rock**: any hard natural material from the Earth.
- **stone**: any hard natural material from the Earth.
- **pebble**: small stone smoothed by water.
- **igneous rock**: rock from inside the Earth itself.
- **sedimentary rock**: eroded rock, carried by water and put down somewhere else.
- **metamorphic rock**: rock that has been changed by heat and pressure.

Beneath our feet

The Earth is like a giant soft-boiled egg. The Earth's core – the yolk of the egg – is incredibly hot and liquid. The Earth's mantle – the white of the egg – surrounds it and is also hot and liquid. It breaks out in places as volcanoes.

The Earth's crust – the shell of the egg – is cold and hard. It is made from solid rock. Wherever you are on Earth, even if you are on a ship in the middle of the sea, there is rock beneath you. You are on solid ground.

Just a minute. The school field isn't rock, nor is the park or the garden. That's because the rock is covered with a layer of earth or soil. If you dig down through this soil, you will find rock under it. Everywhere.

Where soil comes from

The weather transforms rocks. Remember we talked about the fact that when water freezes it expands? Well, even the strongest rock can be split by the 'ice wedge' – water entering cracks in the rock, freezing, expanding and splitting the rock apart. Smaller rocks are acted on by wind and rain, the sea or plant or animal action. Finally, they break down to tiny particles which, mixed with organic matter from plants or animals, make up our soil. Soil is important to plant growth, of course. And plant roots are important for securing the soil against weathering.

A soil profile

We are always digging up the ground. We dig holes to build houses and roads and to lay pipes and cables. If there is some digging near you, you might be able to visit it with a class or a group. Stand somewhere safe. Look into the hole that has been dug. You will see the soil profile.

- **The topsoil**: dark, rich, full of rotting plants.
- **The subsoil**: different in colour; tightly-packed soil.
- **Rocky soil**: a layer of rock that is breaking down to become soil.
- **The bedrock**: this is the rock beneath the soil.

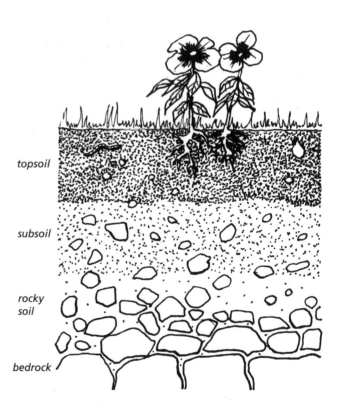

topsoil

subsoil

rocky soil

bedrock

From rock to soil

But where does all this soil come from?

Rock is hard. But when the sun shines on it in the day, it swells up. When it is cold at night, it shrinks away. All this swelling and shrinking breaks bits off it. In the middle of winter, cracks fill up with water. The water freezes and the ice begins to push the rock apart. The ice splits the rock open. The river that sweeps past it bangs rocks against it, knocking off chips of rock.

Eventually, the rock crumbles to stone. The stones are rubbed and banged together by the river. The stones become gravel, then grains of sand, then a fine powder. The powder becomes mixed with bits of rotting plants, living bacteria and tiny fungi that live off the rotting plants, and air and water. The rock becomes soil.

Special soil – clay

Where the soil particles are very fine and suspended in water, the soil is clay. Where the particles are fairly large and can be poured, the soil is sand. Most soils are somewhere between these two. Loam is a mixture of the two and offers a good balance of drainage, security and nutrients to growing plants.

Clay can exist in different forms. Working with clay demonstrates the differences. Which of the forms of clay can be converted or reversed to another? Slip can be dried out, 'leather' pots soaked with water can be remade, but fired pots have been chemically changed and can never return to clay again.

Personal experience of working with clay is helpful here. You need to understand how clay behaves to determine its best use for each possible purpose – from bone china to house bricks.

Clay, like sand, is made up of small particles, but unlike sand, the particles are stuck together with water. Added water trickles into the gaps between the particles to make liquid 'slip'. You need to wet pieces you add to your clay work, otherwise the pieces fall off when dry.

Fascinating facts

- The Chinese were the first to drill into the ground, a thousand years ago. They drilled for water using a seesaw with a chisel roped to one end. By jumping on and off the plank, they dug the chisel into the rock. The same technique was still used in Burma up to 1910.

- A hundred and fifty years ago, tooth powder was made from ground up coral, cuttlefish bone, eggshells or porcelain. Often the powder was coloured either red or purple with cochineal, made from the bodies of tropical insects.

Activities

Level One

Challenge the children to classify the different rocks in a rock set. Ask them to group them by colour, then texture. Ask the children to compare the colours of the rocks in and out of water.

Level Two

Give the children a selection of rocks. Ask them to compare the rocks by seeing which will scratch which. Then ask them to experiment to find out which will mark paper.

Using the results of their experiments, ask the children to put the rocks in order of hardness according to which scratches which. Which is the hardest rock and which the softest?

Level Three

Ask the children to compare different soils. First, ask them to find which will take a shape (clay) and which will not (sand). Then ask them to compare the way that water runs through them by putting them in a filter funnel with a filter paper and pouring water through. Is it possible to roll the soil out as a sausage? To bend the sausage around a curve? These things are possible with clay soils.

Invite the children to use coarse sieves to separate the components in soils. Why should larger hole, coarser sieves be used first? They remove the larger stones, then you can separate the smaller pebbles, the fine sands and the finest particles last.

Level Four

Challenge the children to compare different soils by making measurements of the amount of water that passes through them and working out the amount retained. Help the children to compare these results with other characteristics of the soils.

Ask the children to make a record of different soils and their properties. Compare loam, compost and other soil substitutes. Which holds water best? Pour water through a funnel containing the soil. Measure the water that passes through and compare it with the water used. How much was retained? Clay soils hold more than sandy soils.

Level Five

Ask the children to make a growth comparison between plants. Give them some plant seeds and two or more different soils. Tell them to plant the seeds, and then observe and record the growth. How is growth affected by the different soils?

Use a commercial soil testing kit – with supervision – to find out the differences between the soils. Which are acid and which alkaline? What plants are suited to each soil?

Where does rain come from?

Well, rainwater isn't new. It's been round and round the water cycle since forever. All the Earth's water is trapped in this endless cycle of change. When you drink a glass of water, you can be fairly sure that at least one of the molecules at one time was part of the water drunk by a hero of yours, or by a historical character.

It's statistically likely. It has been estimated that a molecule of water from a glass poured into the sea at Southend in Essex will wash up on the beach in Auckland, New Zealand, in a matter of months. On the way it will have had amazing adventures – as part of the sea, a pond, a river, a cup of tea or a glass of cola.

These adventures are what constitute the water cycle. They are the reason why our water is seldom 'new'. It has always been used before in some way, especially if it is taken from a river. It is estimated that the water in the River Thames has been used by seven people before it reaches the sea, and that includes some of them drinking it.

You don't have to look far to see examples of water cycles all around you. Consider, for example, getting caught out in the rain. When you get home you take off your wet clothes and put them in the washing machine. By the time you have done this, the weather has brightened up, and you hang the clothes outside to dry. The water returns to the sky. These simple actions demonstrate a simple water cycle. While the basic story of the water cycle is the same, the variations are enormous.

Water evaporates

Molecules of water close to the surface are in constant movement. If they have enough energy, they break free of the water and lift into the sky. This can happen at any time. If you leave a saucer of water on a windowsill, meaning to put a pot plant in it later, the water will evaporate at room temperature. By the time you put the pot plant there a day or two later, the water level will have dropped. The water is evaporating.

Evaporation happens much faster if you put a bit of energy into the system. If you heat the water, the molecules get excited and break off with far more regularity. The water may 'steam'. It loses water molecules fast and if you are not careful, it will boil dry. The more energy you apply, the faster the evaporation. Boiling water is losing molecules fast.

While they are above boiling point, the water molecules are actually a gas – water gas. This is true 'steam'. It's invisible and very, very hot. You can see it, or rather, not see it, at the spout of a kettle. But the molecules quickly cool and become cloudy. This is the steam that fills the kitchen or bathroom. It's actually water vapour – water molecules below boiling point, clouding the air.

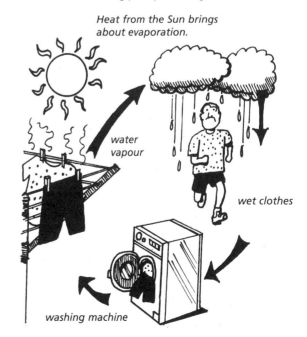

Heat from the Sun brings about evaporation.

water vapour

wet clothes

washing machine

Breezy day

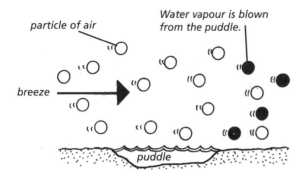

particle of air

Water vapour is blown
from the puddle.

breeze

puddle

Calm day

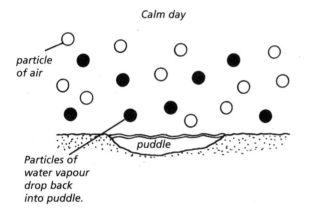

particle
of air

puddle

Particles of
water vapour
drop back
into puddle.

The cloudiness of water vapour is what makes it hard to see on misty days. In the UK, there is a fair amount of water vapour always in the air, and so it is hard to see great distances. When you visit a hot, dry country, you can be astonished by the clarity of distant things and the sharpness of the colours – there is little water vapour in the air to spoil your view.

So the water cycle starts when the water around us – in the seas, rivers, streams, ponds, swimming pools, and even in that saucer on the windowsill – evaporates from the surface and rises into the sky, to form clouds.

There's a big role for trees here, as they pull water from the ground and lose it through their leaves – a process known as transpiration.

A handy spin-off of this evaporation process is that the water that rises into the atmosphere is clean. It has left all its impurities behind. There are even rings of impurity left on that saucer. The pure water has gone up to form clouds.

What's in a cloud?

You have probably flown through a cloud if you have taken a foreign holiday. But you have also walked through one if you have seen a mist or fog on the ground. Both clouds and mist are made up of water vapour, condensed into minute water particles that float in the atmosphere or roll across the hills.

As the water vapour rises, it cools, and it clumps or condenses, often around tiny dust particles. The 'smogs' of the big cities are caused by water condensing around the waste from fires or car exhausts.

There are many different types of clouds, classified by their shape and the height at which they are found. Some contain minute ice crystals.

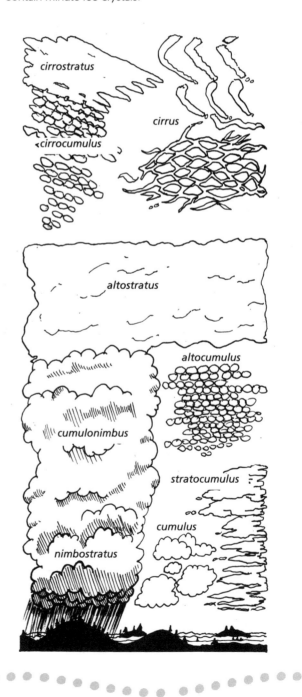

cirrostratus

cirrus

cirrocumulus

altostratus

altocumulus

cumulonimbus

stratocumulus

cumulus

nimbostratus

Down came the rain

Clouds are unstable. As they rise and cool, the water condenses. Droplets run together to form bigger and bigger drops. Finally these drops are so big that they can no longer hang in the air, and they fall as rain.

Condensing is the process of combining the water molecules. You see it taking place in your bathroom. Reaching a cold surface, water vapour from your shower condenses into water droplets, and these run down the mirror or window. We call the stuff (incorrectly) condensation. In fact it is condensed water. The process is condensation.

Up in the clouds, the condensed water droplets start to fall. Because this usually happens at quite a height, it is more likely to occur in mountainous or hilly places, or close to them. So the Lancashire mill towns, where a wet atmosphere was helpful to the management of fabrics and fibres, are close to the Pennines.

If clouds are carried by the wind over high ground, they may rise higher and higher, getting colder and colder. The water vapour freezes (snow is frozen vapour, not frozen liquid) and a crystal of ice is formed in these high clouds. As up-draughts push the clouds higher still, more water vapour joins the crystals, and when they are too heavy to be suspended any longer, they fall as snow. If more water gathers round the frozen particle, it forms a hailstone.

Rivers and streams

Once it's fallen as rain, the water's journey is far from over. Many possibilities arise. A droplet of rain may join a stream or river. It may soak into the ground, only to pop up somewhere else in a spring or well. It may scarcely touch the Earth, hardly arriving before it evaporates away again.

Or it may start a long adventure that includes pushing round a turbine to generate electricity, being boiled for a cup of tea, passing through one or more humans, being cleaned in a sewage-farm, falling through a shower head, and being mixed with a measure of Scotch. It may wash your car, water your garden or boil your potatoes. It may be drawn into a plant and combined with oxygen to produce more plant material and so food for animals. Eventually it may find itself back in the sea. And the whole cycle begins again.

A drop of water may travel thousands of kilometres between the time it evaporates and the time it falls to Earth again as rain or snow. On the way, it may be partly responsible for some extreme weather conditions.

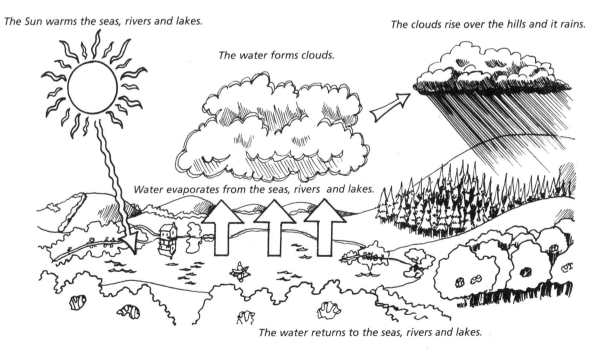

The Sun warms the seas, rivers and lakes.

The clouds rise over the hills and it rains.

The water forms clouds.

Water evaporates from the seas, rivers and lakes.

The water returns to the seas, rivers and lakes.

Storms

Thunderstorms are heavy storms with rain, thunder and lightning. We usually get them in the summer because then the ground gets hot and the rising warm air forms tall clouds with a flat 'anvil' top. Electricity crackles in these clouds, caused by water particles rubbing together. When the charge has built up it snaps to the ground as a flash of lightning. The air heated by the lightning flash creates shock waves that we hear as thunder.

Lightning travels at 140,000km per second. That's half the speed of light. While the streak is very narrow (less than 2cm wide), it can be 43km long. You can survive being hit by lightning as long as it goes to Earth without passing through your heart. Park ranger Roy Sullivan claimed to have been hit by lightning seven times between 1942 and 1977.

Thunderclouds can grow to be ten to twelve miles high. Their anvil shape is caused by high winds at that height, blowing the top sideways. Some of the water in them stays unfrozen, even at minus 40°C. But clouds also contain fragments of ice that are growing onion-like, layer by layer. They then may become too heavy to be held up by currents of air and so fall to the ground as hail. If the air currents are really fast (as much as 145kph), the hailstones may grow to the size of oranges before they drop from the cloud.

Counting the seconds between flash and bang can give you an idea of the distance between you and a storm. Allow three seconds for a kilometre; five seconds for a mile.

Fascinating facts

- Tutunendo in Colombia is the rainiest place on Earth, with 1,179 cm of rain a year.

- 25cm of snow melts to 2.5cm water on average.

- There are records of raining frogs. More unusual showers reported have included fish, spiders, snails and turtles. Waterspouts (funnel-shaped columns of water drawn from the surface of water by very high winds) are usually blamed.

- In some parts of the world, the clouds are permanent, creating an amazing environment called a cloud forest.

Floods

Flash floods are the weather's biggest killer. They are extremely difficult to forecast, and they may be very localised. On 31 July 1976, huge thunderclouds formed along the edge of the Rocky Mountains in Colorado, USA. There were no strong winds to slice their tops off, and they reached over 21,000 metres in height. That evening, they dropped 30.5cm of rain into the Big Thompson River. This was in an area that normally receives only 40.5cm of rain a year. Water poured down the rocky valley, sweeping pine trees, boulders, houses and cars before it, and killing 239 people.

On 15 August 1952, a flash flood hit the Devon village of Lynmouth after three months' worth of rain fell in 24 hours. Ninety-three buildings were destroyed and all the 28 bridges across the two Lyn rivers were swept away. Thirty-four people were killed as three billion gallons of water flowed through the village in one night.

Yet neither of these can compare with the flooding that could result from global warming. Carbon dioxide and other greenhouse gases from power stations, industry, the burning of rainforests and vehicles of all sorts, are forming a blanket around the Earth that traps the Sun's heat instead of allowing it to reflect into space. The Earth is getting warmer.

As the Earth gets warmer, the sea level is rising, both through expansion and because ice caps are melting. A rise of one metre in sea level will flood a third of Bangladesh, a low-lying country, making two hundred million people homeless.

Droughts and deserts

A lack of water can be just as devastating. Nomadic peoples live from the land in one area and then move on, allowing the land to recover naturally. For these people, the change to settlement and crop-growing has brought its own problems. The reuse of land can break down the soil structure. Clearing trees to farm, or to use or burn the timber, leaves huge areas open to erosion and without the roots that once caged the soil.

The UK has seen the results on a very small scale in East Anglia where giant fields were created by the removal of hedgerows to allow the entry of large farm machines. Wildlife is affected, and hedge-nesting birds are lost. In parts of Africa, 'jessours' (low banks) have been built to retain the soil and protect irrigated areas.

When drought conditions combine with conflict, as in parts of Africa, millions die.

Hurricanes and tornadoes

A hurricane (called a typhoon in the Northern Pacific and a cyclone in the Indian Ocean) originates close to the equator when a central calm 'eye' is surrounded by inwardly spiralling winds. As the sea temperature rises, water evaporates into whirling, unstable storm clouds. A hurricane is a wind of force 12 or more on the Beaufort scale, and is accompanied by lightning and torrential rain. Hurricane Gilbert in the Caribbean in 1988 gusted up to 320kph. A cyclone in the Bay of Bengal in November 1970 caused the sea to rise ten metres, crashing into the Ganges delta to drown at least 300,000 people and one million farm animals.

The UK doesn't experience hurricanes, though sometimes we like to think that we do. While south-east England felt the strongest winds there for 300 years in October 1987 and January 1990, they were nowhere near hurricane force.

We would be mistaken to think that we can afford to neglect – or to think we can manage – the weather. Science can help us to understand the world but we can easily underestimate the power of natural forces.

Activities

Level One

Ask the children to draw round a puddle in the playground with chalk – this could either be a rain puddle or one made by pouring water into a hollow in the tarmac. Tell the children to return every hour throughout the day to see how the puddle has changed. On each return visit, they should chalk a new border. The children may think that the water is sinking into the ground – show them, by pouring smaller amounts of water on it, that tarmac is waterproof.

Do the same activity with containers of water in the classroom. Where has the water gone?

Level Two

Ask the children to collect the rain daily. They could use a rain gauge or make their own by using a wide funnel that empties into a jar or other container. They should pour the water collected into a measuring jug or cylinder. The narrower the measure, the greater the differences between the levels for each day. The children could either cork these amounts and keep them for direct comparison, build a bar-chart with Unifix cubes, or record the rainfall as a bar-chart. Use the records for prediction. Can you predict the weather or the rainfall?

Level Three

Set up an investigation into evaporation. Ask the children to find out whether the size or surface area of a container affects the speed of evaporation. Also ask them to investigate whether the place you put the liquid affects the speed of evaporation. It's raining indoors!

Level Four

Relate evaporation to heat, and explore condensation (teacher only) using a boiling kettle and a cold surface. As the kettle boils (you may need to hold a thermostatic switch on), let the water vapour condense on a cold surface – like a jar containing ice. Use this experience to help the children place evaporation and condensation in the water cycle.

The children can copy this experiment– using water that is hot but safe – by putting the water in a bowl and covering it with clingfilm. Tell them to put a few ice cubes on the film, so that the film dips and is cool. Evaporated water will condense on it and drip back into the bowl.

Level Five

Link the states of matter and the water cycle by taking water through all the different states – ice, water and vapour – and comparing and contrasting what happens at each stage. How is it possible to begin with an ice cube and end with one, after water has been through its two other states?

Put a little water in a polythene bag and seal it. Tape it to the window and observe it through the day. You will have a 'cloud in a bag' and can observe the whole water cycle.

Test the rainfall with a universal indicator or litmus paper. Compare the acidity with that of lemon juice and vinegar. Ask the children to research 'acid rain' and its effects on forests and buildings.